Alternate Route

CLIFFORD WINSTON *and*
CHAD SHIRLEY

Alternate Route

Toward Efficient Urban Transportation

BROOKINGS INSTITUTION PRESS
Washington, D.C.

Copyright © 1998 by

THE BROOKINGS INSTITUTION
1775 Massachusetts Avenue, N.W.
Washington, D.C. 20036

Library of Congress Cataloging-in-Publication data

Winston, Clifford, 1951–
    Alternate route : toward efficient urban transportation /
Clifford Winston and Chad Shirley.
    p. cm.
    Includes bibliographical references and index.

    ISBN 0-8157-9382-0 (cloth : alk. paper)
    ISBN 0-8157-9381-2 (pbk : alk. paper)
    1. Urban transportation policy—United States.   2. Urban
transportation—United States—Planning.   3. Urban
transportation—United States—Cost effectiveness. 4. Traffic
congestion—United States.   I. Shirley, Chad.   II. Title.
   HE308 .W56 1998
   388.4'0973--ddc21   98-25419
                                        CIP

9 8 7 6 5 4 3 2 1

The paper used in this publication meets the minimum requirements of the American National
Standard for Information Sciences—Permanence of Paper for Printed Library Materials,
ANSI Z39.48-1984

Typeset in Times Roman

Composition by R. Lynn Rivenbark
Macon, Georgia

Printed by R. R. Donnelly and Sons
Harrisonburg, Virginia

Foreword

M ANY U.S. URBAN AREAS are characterized by severe highway congestion, deteriorating bus operations that run heavy deficits, and strong pressures to build or expand rail systems. Popular solutions to these problems often call for large increases in public spending on urban transportation. In this study Clifford Winston and Chad Shirley present a comprehensive solution to urban transportation problems based on promoting competition and efficiency. The authors first estimate that inefficient prices, service, and operations are costing society considerably more than $10 billion (1990 dollars) annually. They find that these costs stem from entrenched and powerful political forces that fail to systematically advance any recognizable social goal. The authors' solution is for policymakers to experiment with shielding urban transportation from these political forces by privatizing transit systems, deregulating taxis, and promoting private tollways. These experiments, if conducted carefully, should open up entire urban transportation systems to competition and stimulate operators to offer efficient service that is responsive to travelers' preferences.

Clifford Winston is senior fellow in the Brookings Economic Studies program, and Chad Shirley is a former research assistant in the Brookings Economic Studies program. The authors are grateful to Linda Cohen and Carole Uhlaner for initial discussions that helped shape this study. They are also grateful to many people for their helpful suggestions and comments, including John Chubb, Thomas Corsi, Robert Crandall, Anthony Downs, José Gomez-Ibañez, Alfred Kahn, John Kain, Robert Litan, Fred Mannering, John Meyer, Michael Meyer, Steven Morrison, Pietro Nivola, Don Pickrell, Kenneth Small, Kenneth Train, Philip Viton, and Tara Watson. They also benefited from comments received at seminars at the

University of Chicago and the World Bank. Research assistance was provided by Tara Watson and Karen McClure.

James Schneider and Brenda Szittya edited the manuscript, Jennifer Eichberger verified its factual content, Mariah Seagle proofread the pages, and Sherry Smith prepared the index.

The views expressed in this book are those of the authors and should not be ascribed to those persons or organizations whose assistance is acknowledged or to the trustees, officers, or other staff members of the Brookings Institution.

MICHAEL H. ARMACOST
President

August 1998
Washington, D.C.

Contents

1

Introduction and Overview

STUDENTS TAKING the Ph.D. qualifying examination in transportation economics at the University of California, Berkeley, were asked the following question:

You are appointed to an all-powerful position of transportation czar in a medium-large American metropolitan area. It faces what the press terms a severe urban transportation problem, taking on the following characteristics: radial highways are jammed during rush hours, so commuters suffer considerable delays relative to non–rush hour travelers; bus service, never fast, has deteriorated over the years; and fares have risen considerably. Still, the bus operation runs heavy deficits. Although rail transit service was abandoned years ago for lack of patronage, there are now strong pressures from various quarters to build a new fixed rail system.

Assuming this is an economic problem, sketch out the way you would use economic analysis to solve it conceptually.

Established economists, it seems, think they know how to solve America's urban transportation problems. But this examination question was asked in 1976, and despite the zeal with which veterans of examinations past have tackled the question, the problems that it describes have grown worse.

Part of the difficulty in finding a solution lies in assuming that the problem is solely an economic one to be solved within the public sector. The contention of this book is that policymakers' political objectives have led to urban transportation's economic problems. The solution to these problems therefore lies in minimizing policymakers' influence on the system's performance. This can only be accomplished by allowing the private sector to assume a primary role in providing transportation in America's cities.

Public Sector Involvement in Urban Transportation

In the late 1950s federal policymakers began to focus on urban issues and consider policies to address them. Public officials from New York, Chicago, Philadelphia, and other large cities strongly advocated major federal funding of mass transportation systems on the grounds that it would be an effective stimulant to urban renewal.[1] The 1961 Housing Act gave cities $75 million to buy transit companies that had been losing customers and deteriorating financially for years. In 1964 the Urban Mass Transportation Act signaled the start of major federal funding of transit (bus and rail) capital expenditures. The federal government had set a precedent of subsidizing urban transportation by funding urban extensions of the interstate highway system, and some big-city mayors argued that subsidizing transit was more cost effective than subsidizing more highways.

There was also a debate over the form of federal funding.[2] The states wanted federal funds to flow through them. They in turn would contract with private bus and rail operators for specified services (before the mid-1960s most urban transit systems were private), and the industry would continue to remain largely private rather than become publicly owned. In contrast, an alliance of big-city mayors, other urban advocates, financially strapped transit operators, and railroads trying to shed commuter service as part of a larger effort to end passenger service wanted federal support to go

---

1. Comprehensive overviews of the development of urban transportation systems, their economic problems, and policy initiatives can be found in John R. Meyer, John F. Kain, and Martin Wohl, *The Urban Transportation Problem* (Harvard University Press, 1965); Alan A. Altshuler, with James P. Womak and John R. Pucher, *The Urban Transportation System: Politics and Policy Innovation* (MIT Press, 1979); John R. Meyer and José Gomez-Ibañez, *Autos, Transit, and Cities* (Harvard University Press, 1981); David W. Jones, *Urban Transit Policy: An Economic and Political History* (Prentice-Hall, 1985); and John F. Kain, "The Urban Transportation Problem: A Reexamination and Update," in José A. Gomez-Ibañez, William B. Tye, and Clifford Winston, eds., *Essays in Transportation Economics and Policy: A Handbook in Honor of John R. Meyer* (Brookings, 1998).

2. Jones, *Urban Transit Policy*.

directly to operators or cities that owned or were soon to own municipal transit systems. For the most part this coalition prevailed, and publicly owned transit systems proliferated. Public ownership increased from 88 systems in 1965, which accounted for 44 percent of all transit vehicles, to 333 systems in 1975, or more than 85 percent of all transit vehicles.[3]

During the same period federal capital grants grew from $50 million to $1.3 billion. In 1973 the House and Senate Public Works Committees added mass transit to their long-standing jurisdiction over highway construction and made massive amounts of federal funding, which had been earmarked for highway construction, available to local governments to expand mass transit. The resulting adversarial relationship between highway and transit interests persists today. Of course, this conflict and the current problems in transit systems may have been far different had the states had greater influence over the form of federal funding and had transit remained in private hands.

Well before federal capital grants were introduced in 1964, the automobile had been displacing motor bus and light rail systems (trolleys and streetcars).[4] The growth in federal support of mass transit halted the decline in motor bus and light rail use and by the 1970s fueled an expansion in bus and heavy rail capacity (figure 1-1).[5] Today, bus capacity appears to be peaking, but with many cities planning to build new light rail systems or

---

3. American Public Transit Association (APTA), *Transit Fact Book* (Washington, annual).

4. Although the automobile was an important factor in the decline of these alternative forms of transportation, Peter B. Pashigian, "Consequences and Causes of Public Ownership of Urban Transit Facilities," *Journal of Political Economy*, vol. 84 (December 1976), pp. 1239–59, and George W. Hilton, "The Rise and Fall of Monopolized Transit," in Charles Lave, ed., *Urban Transit: The Private Challenge to Public Transportation* (Cambridge, Mass.: Ballinger, 1985), pp. 31–48, argue that government regulation also contributed to the decline of bus operations.

5. Heavy rail is defined as an electric railway with the capacity for a "heavy volume" of traffic. It is characterized by exclusive rights-of-way, multicar trains, high speed, rapid acceleration, sophisticated signaling, and loading passengers from raised platforms. Other names include subway, elevated railway, and metropolitan railway (metro). Light rail is defined as an electric railway with a "light volume" of traffic. It may use exclusive or shared rights of way, high or low platform loading, and multicar trains or single cars. Other names include streetcar, trolley, and tramway. It would be preferable to measure bus and rail capacity in terms of seat miles instead of vehicle miles. Unfortunately, we were only able to obtain information from the American Public Transit Association on seat miles since 1980. Based on these data, bus and heavy rail seating capacity has remained relatively constant, while light rail's seating capacity has increased somewhat. Thus, using vehicle miles instead of seat miles understates the recent growth of light rail capacity but does not have much impact on the growth of bus and heavy rail capacity.

Figure 1-1. *Heavy and Light Rail and Motor Bus Vehicle Miles, 1950–95*[a]

Vehicle miles (billions)

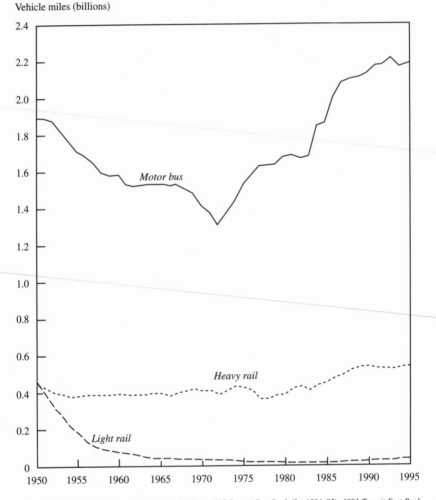

Sources: American Public Transit Association (APTA), *1997 Transit Fact Book* (for 1984–95); *1991 Transit Fact Book* (for 1975–83); *1974–75 Transit Fact Book* (for 1960–73); *1981 Transit Fact Book* (for 1974); and *Transit Fact Book 1960* (for 1950–59).

a. A number of smaller and rural systems are excluded before 1984.

extend their heavy or light rail systems, heavy rail capacity is likely to continue to grow and light rail capacity could grow considerably.

Although public transit capacity has grown nationwide, during the past fifteen years many cities' systems have cut bus service frequency, and New York, Chicago, and San Francisco have cut rail service frequency and raised real transit fares (table 1-1). Indeed, since 1980 real average transit fares have increased 44 percent.[6] According to critics of public transit, these trends are not surprising because as much as 75 percent of federal spending on transit actually accrues to transit operators and the suppliers of transit capital, while only 25 percent is used to improve service and reduce fares.[7]

Despite considerable government support, public transit has failed to lure urban travelers from their cars. In fact, since the 1960s bus and rail system patronage and mode shares for work trips have diminished. Rising incomes and growth in the number of suburban workplaces and residences have stimulated commuters' preferences for traveling in their automobiles, causing autos' share of work trips to climb to nearly 84 percent by 1990 (table 1-2). Between 1960 and 1990, transit's share of *all* trips in large urban areas fell from more than 20 percent to less than 10 percent.[8] The dramatic shrinkage in transit's share at the national level may not be readily apparent because of its large patronage in a few major cities and its heavy peak-period ridership on some major urban corridors throughout the country.

Urban Transportation Problems

The major economic problems facing today's urban transportation systems include large transit deficits, the proliferation of expensive rail systems, automobile congestion and the costs of expanding highway capacity, vehicle pollution and safety, and adequate accessibility to jobs and recreational activities.

---

6. Average U.S. transit fares per passenger mile (in 1990 dollars) were 10.2 cents in 1980 and 15.1 cents in 1994. These figures are calculated with data from American Public Transit Association, *Transit Fact Book* (1992, 1998).

7. See, for example, Don H. Pickrell, "Rising Deficits and the Uses of Transit Subsidies in the United States," *Journal of Transport Economics and Policy*, vol. 19 (September 1985), pp. 281–98; and Douglass B. Lee, *Evaluation of Federal Transit Operating Subsidies* (Cambridge, Mass.: Transportation Systems Center, Department of Transportation, September 1987), p. 2. Pickrell points out that some of the factors that divert federal subsidies, such as part of the growth in wage rates, were outside the control of the transit industry.

8. Passenger counts and mode shares for all types of trips are available from Federal Highway Administration, *Nationwide Personal Transportation Survey* (Department of Transportation, 1990). Because the sample sizes are generally considered small, national estimates derived from these data should be regarded as preliminary. Nonetheless, the data reveal trends and magnitudes that are consistent with those based on reliable samples of work trips.

Table 1-1. *Bus and Rail Service and Transit Fares, Selected Transit Systems, 1980–94*

City and transit system (1990 name of system) and modal attribute	1980	1990	1994	Percent change 1980–94
New York—MTA-NYCTA				
Bus frequency (revenue vehicle miles per directional route mile per hour)	5.9	5.8	5.6	−5.1
Rail frequency (revenue vehicle miles per directional route mile per hour)	126.3	71.4	69.5	−45.0
Average fare per trip (1990 dollars)	0.55	0.70	0.78	41.5
Average fare per mile (1990 dollars)	0.17	0.19	0.21	29.7
Chicago—RTA-CTA				
Bus frequency (revenue vehicle miles per directional route mile per hour)	6.3	6.0	6.0	−4.8
Rail frequency (revenue vehicle miles per directional route mile per hour)	32.4	33.8	25.1	−22.5
Average fare per trip (1990 dollars)	0.48	0.57	0.67	39.6
Average fare per mile (1990 dollars)	0.14	0.17	0.19	33.3
Boston—MBTA				
Bus frequency (revenue vehicle miles per directional route mile per hour)	1.9	1.8	1.8	−5.3
Rail frequency (revenue vehicle miles per directional route mile per hour)	10.9	21.7	22.0	101.8
Average fare per trip (1990 dollars)	0.43	0.42	0.42	−0.9
Average fare per mile (1990 dollars)	0.17	0.15	0.12	−28.9
San Francisco—Muni				
Bus frequency (revenue vehicle miles per directional route mile per hour)	3.8	3.2	3.2	−15.8
Rail frequency (revenue vehicle miles per directional route mile per hour)	11.0	9.4	8.3	−24.5
Average fare per trip (1990 dollars)	0.28	0.33	0.39	39.9
Average fare per mile (1990 dollars)	0.15	0.17	0.20	36.3
Pittsburgh—PAT				
Bus frequency (revenue vehicle miles per directional route mile per hour)	1.7	1.2	1.1	−35.3
Rail frequency (revenue vehicle miles per directional route mile per hour)	4.8	4.0	4.9	2.1
Average fare per trip (1990 dollars)	0.70	0.58	0.61	−13.2
Average fare per mile (1990 dollars)	0.16	0.13	0.15	−8.7

Sources: Department of Transportation, 1981 Section 15 database; 1990 Section 15 database; 1994 Section 15 database; authors' calculations. Data for 1980 collected for fiscal years ending between July 1980 and June 1981 and reported as 1981 Section 15 database; 1990 data collected for fiscal years ending in the 1990 calendar year; and 1994 data collected for fiscal years ending in the 1994 calendar year.

Table 1-2. *Commuting Passengers and Mode Shares, Urban Areas Exceeding 1 Million Population, 1960, 1970, 1980, 1990*

Item and mode	1960	1970	1980	1990
Primary means of commuting (millions of workers)				
Privately owned vehicle	17.5	27.6	36.5	49.8
Bus	3.8	3.3	3.0	2.9
Subway/rail	2.3	2.2	2.0	2.3
Walk	3.0	2.7	2.1	2.2
Other	2.2	1.2	1.7	2.4
Commuting (percent of workers)				
Privately owned vehicle	61.0	74.4	80.4	83.5
Bus	13.1	9.0	6.7	4.9
Subway/rail	8.0	5.9	4.5	3.8
Walk	10.4	7.4	4.7	3.8
Other	7.5	3.3	3.7	4.0

Sources: Data for 1980 and 1990 from Federal Highway Administration, *Journey-to-Work Trends in the United States and Its Major Metropolitan Areas, 1960–1990* (Department of Transportation, 1993), tables 5-6 and 5-6A; data for 1960 and 1970 are from Federal Highway Administration, "Journey-to-Work Trends Based on 1960, 1970, and 1980 Decennial Census" (July 1986), tables 6-1 and 6-6; and authors' calculations.

Note: The "other" category in 1960 and 1970 passenger trips includes walking, taxi, motorcycle, bicycle, and respondents who work at home. The "other" category in 1980 and 1990 and in mode share includes these modes except walking. The mode share data for walking in 1960 and 1970 are based on U.S. data rather than major urban area data. The major urban areas with population exceeding 1 million changes by decade.

Transit Deficits

The long-run growth in transit capacity, spurred by federal subsidies, and the long-run decline in transit's share of travelers, caused by growing use of the automobile and accelerated by rising real fares and the decreasing frequency of service, have combined to make public transit's financial deficits a serious drain on the public purse. In the 1960s, transit programs were given capital assistance, which could not be used to defray operating costs. This requirement was eliminated in the 1970s as the programs proliferated across the nation, partly in response to the energy crisis of 1973–74, and operating deficits started to grow. Federal operating subsidies for transit began in 1974. By 1995, public transit in the United States was saddled with about $18 billion in annual operating expenses while generating only $9.6 billion in operating revenues (figure 1-2).[9] The operating

9. Separate data for rail and bus operating expenses and operating revenues have been available since 1990. Based on these data, bus operations, which constitute 62 percent of transit passenger miles, are responsible for nearly two-thirds of the transit operating deficit. The total deficit from transit operations would be higher if we accounted for capital investments. In 1995 these were nearly $7 billion. American Public Transit Association, *1998 Transit Fact Book*, table 11.

Figure 1-2. *Real Transit Operating Revenues and Expenses, 1950–95*[a]

Billions of 1995 dollars

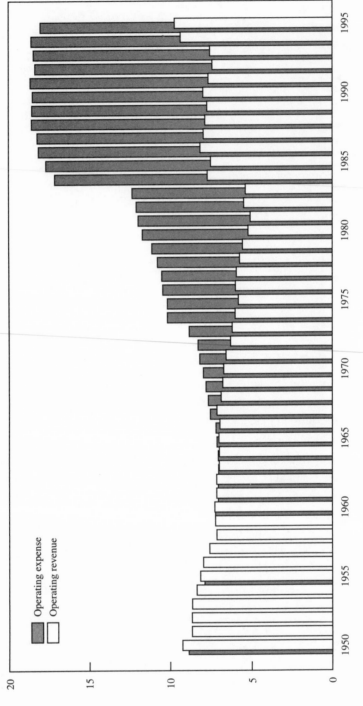

Source: APTA, *Transit Fact Book* (1960, 1974–75, 1977–79, 1990, 1991, 1996).

a. Commuter rail, automated guideway, urban ferry boat, demand response, and a number of smaller and rural systems are excluded before 1984. Fares retained by contractors are included in operating revenue after 1983. Depreciation costs are excluded from operating expenses after 1974. Data were not available for operating expenses in 1951–54 and 1956–59.

subsidies per passenger trip amounted to $1.45 for bus, $.99 for light rail, and $.74 for heavy rail. Assuming that the average annual number of work trips for commuters (508) is the same for all modes, the average annual work trip operating subsidy is $737 for each bus commuter, $503 for light rail commuters, and $376 for heavy rail commuters. Given that the average 1995 household income of bus commuters approached $40,000 and the average 1995 household income of rail commuters exceeded $50,000, these subsidies cannot be justified primarily as redistributing income to the working poor.[10]

Because real costs per trip continue to rise, many state and local governments are trying to limit the growth in transit spending and have proposed cutting service on the most unprofitable routes in their systems and raising fares. Those cities that are not raising fares or cutting service are being forced to contribute more funds to their region's transit system.[11] Since the late 1980s, federal and local governments have cut back real operating assistance to mass transit, forcing the states to bear a greater share of the financial responsibility for their transit systems (table 1-3). States have also increased their share of capital assistance.

In 1997, initial debates over federal funding for mass transit and highway spending, prompted by the reauthorization of the 1991 Intermodal Surface Transportation Efficiency Act (ISTEA) legislation, focused on how much financial assistance could be reduced. A new transportation bill was postponed, however, until 1998, during which time Congress felt less pressure to curb transportation spending because of actual and projected improvements in the federal budget. The result was the Transportation Equity Act for the 21st Century, which substantially increases federal

10. Operating subsidies are authors' calculations based on data from APTA, *1998 Transit Fact Book*, tables 22 and 30. Average number of work trips and average incomes of bus and rail commuters are calculated from the Federal Highway Administration, 1995 *Nationwide Personal Transportation Survey*.

11. To take some examples, the Fairfax County Board of Supervisors in Northern Virginia was presented with a proposal that would reduce or eliminate service on twenty-six routes to save the county $2.2 million; see Tod Robberson, "Bus Users Fear Planned Cuts," *Washington Post*, February 22, 1996, Virginia section, p. 1. The Washington Metro agency developed a plan whereby Washington, D.C., would have to contribute more money to the region's transit system to prevent Metro rail and bus riders from facing fare increases or service cuts; see Alice Reid, "Metro Budget Easier on Riders Than on D.C.," *Washington Post*, December 20, 1996, p. C6.

Table 1-3. *Operating and Capital Funding for Mass Transit, by Level of Government, 1986–95*

Constant 1995 dollars unless otherwise specified

Type of funding	1986	1987	1988	1989	1990	1991	1992	1993	1994	1995
Operating assistance (billions)										
Federal	1.309	1.281	1.166	1.151	1.131	1.070	1.053	1.019	0.942	0.817
State	3.206	3.441	3.449	3.437	3.464	3.580	4.214	3.907	3.964	3.830
Local	5.902	6.279	6.304	6.140	6.211	6.013	5.722	5.791	4.289	3.981
Percent of total government operating assistance										
Federal	13	12	11	11	10	10	10	10	10	9
State	31	31	32	32	32	34	38	36	43	44
Local	57	57	58	57	57	56	52	54	47	46
Capital assistance (billions)										
Federal	n.a.	n.a.	3.246	2.982	3.349	3.103	2.904	2.565	2.697	3.422
State	n.a.	n.a.	0.631	0.818	0.812	0.778	0.870	1.398	1.077	1.020
Local	n.a.	n.a.	0.991	0.986	1.372	1.133	0.902	1.139	1.026	0.888
Percent of total government capital assistance										
Federal	n.a.	n.a.	67	62	61	62	62	50	56	64
State	n.a.	n.a.	13	17	15	16	19	27	22	19
Local	n.a.	n.a.	20	21	25	23	19	22	21	17

Source: APTA, *1998 Transit Fact Book*, pp. 38, 52; and authors' calculations.

n.a. Not available.

support for transit and highways from 1998 to 2003.[12] This additional support, however, does not constitute a solution to chronic transit deficits. In fact, it delays the search for one.

New Rail Systems

Technologically sophisticated infrastructure projects such as bridges, buildings, and rail systems have long been a source of civic pride despite their expense. Thus while all signs point to some reduction in local and state government support for existing transit systems, many cities are planning to build light rail systems or to extend their existing systems (table 1-4). Experience has shown, however, that rail ridership tends to be grossly overestimated at the planning stage, especially by rail advocates, while capital and operating costs tend to be significantly underestimated.[13] Indeed, capital and operating costs for heavy rail systems have exceeded estimates by as much as 80 percent and 200 percent, respectively (table 1-5). It has even been argued that forecast errors were intentionally made to gain federal support for proposed projects.[14] The tendency for urban rail systems to expand also makes it difficult to forecast how much a system will cost when its network is fully completed. For example, the proposed network of light rail and subway lines in Los Angeles is projected to cost $75 billion over the next twenty years, but that figure could grow significantly as the system evolves.[15] The enormous projected cost has caused some Los Angeles public officials to call for a halt to building any more of this system. Building new rail systems and extending old ones will probably add substantially to the financial

12. The legislation authorizes some $215 billion in federal transportation spending over the six years. This is a substantial increase over the 1991 ISTEA legislation that authorized $150 billion in transportation spending for 1991–97.

13. For evidence of exaggerated rail ridership forecasts see Melvin M. Webber, "The BART Experience: What Have We Learned?" *Public Interest*, vol. 45 (Fall 1976), pp. 79–108; John F. Kain, "Deception in Dallas: Strategic Misrepresentation in Rail Transit Promotion and Evaluation," *Journal of the American Planning Association*, vol. 56 (Spring 1990), pp. 184–96; and Donald H. Pickrell, "A Desire Named Streetcar: Fantasy and Fact in Rail Transit Planning," *Journal of the American Planning Association*, vol. 58 (Spring 1992), pp. 158–76.

14. Martin Wachs, "Ethics and Advocacy in Forecasting for Public Policy," *Business and Professional Ethics Journal*, vol. 9 (Spring 1990), pp. 141–57.

15. Todd S. Purdum, "The Subway to Nowhere, No Time Soon," *New York Times*, August 28, 1997, p. A1.

Table 1-4. *Cities Planning to Build or Extend Rail Systems, as of October 1996*[a]

City	Characteristics and status
Building new heavy rail	
None	
Building new light rail	
Atlanta	14.5 miles proposed
Hartford	16.3 miles in planning phase, more than half expected to be open by 2000
Kansas City	15.2 miles in planning or design phases
Miami	9.6 miles in planning phase, some expected to be open by 2005
Milwaukee	22.0 miles in planning phase
New York	10.6 miles in planning or design phases, expected to be open by 2001
Norfolk	10.0 miles in planning phases
Oklahoma City	9.1 miles proposed or in planning phase, expected to be open by 2001
Orlando	24.0 miles in planning phase
Salt Lake City	15.8 miles in design phase, expected to be open by 2000
Tampa	2.3 miles in planning phase, expected to be open by 1999
Extending heavy rail	
Atlanta	12.6 miles in planning or design phases
Cleveland	3.0 miles in planning phases
Los Angeles	40.7 miles in planning, planned, design or construction phases, most expected to be open by 2003
Miami	37.6 miles in planning or design phases
New York	0.4 miles in construction phase
San Francisco	62.0 miles proposed, or in planning, design, or construction phases
Washington, D.C.	41.3 miles in planning or construction phases
Extending light rail	
Baltimore	7.3 miles in construction phase, expected to be open by 1997
Boston	2.1 miles proposed
Buffalo	28.6 miles proposed or in planning phase, most expected to be open after 2020
Cleveland	2.0 miles in planning phase
Dallas	48.8 miles proposed or in planning, design, or construction phases, most expected to be open by 2003
Denver	8.7 miles in design phase, expected to be open by 2000
Los Angeles	16.4 miles in planning or construction phases, most expected to be open by 2001
Memphis	4.4 miles in planning or construction phases, expected to open by 1999
New Orleans	7.9 miles proposed or in design phase, expected to open by 2002
New York (NJ Transit)	28.8 miles in planning or design phases
Pittsburgh	5.2 miles in planning phase
Portland	39.0 miles in design or construction phases, some expected to be open in 1998
Sacramento	36.6 miles in planning, design, or construction phases, some expected to be open in 1998
St. Louis	66.6 miles proposed or in planning or design phases, most expected to be open by 2005
San Diego	21.8 miles in planning or construction phases, some expected to be open by 1997
San Francisco	34.0 miles in planning, design, or construction phases
San Jose	27.7 miles in planning, design, or construction phases, most expected to be open by 2003
Seattle	26.6 miles in planning phase, expected to be open by 2004

Source: APTA, *1996 Transit Fixed Guideway Inventory* (Washington, 1996), tables 13 and 19.

a. Projects without specific track mileage and commuter rail projects are excluded. Mileage is approximate one-way mileage.

Table 1-5. *Forecasts and Actual Capital and Operating Costs of*
U.S. Transit Systems, by Type, Selected Cities

Millions of 1988 dollars unless otherwise specified

	Capital costs			Annual operating costs		
System	Forecast	Actual	Difference (percent)	Forecast	Actual	Difference (percent)
Heavy rail						
Washington	4,352	7,968	83	66.3	199.9	202
Atlanta	1,723	2,720	58	13.2	40.3	205
Baltimore	804	1,289	60	. . .	21.7	. . .
Miami	1,008	1,341	33	26.5	37.5	42
Light rail						
Buffalo	478	722	51	10.4	11.6	12
Pittsburgh	699	622	−11	. . .	8.1	. . .
Portland	172	266	55	3.8	5.8	45
Sacramento	165	188	13	7.7	6.9	−10

Source: Don Pickrell, *Forecast versus Actual Ridership and Costs* (Department of Transportation, Urban Rail Transit Projects, 1989), pp. 33, 46.

burden that transit places on the public and will partially offset any efforts to reduce existing deficits.

Highway Costs and Automobile Congestion

With its current share of all urban trips at 90 percent, the automobile has become more than ever the dominant form of urban transportation in the United States.[16] The public has invested hundreds of billions of dollars in building and maintaining roads to accommodate auto travel, but like rail investments, the cost of some of these has turned out to be much greater than anticipated. The most recent and perhaps most glaring example of cost overruns in road building is the so-called Big Dig depression of Boston's central artery, currently expected to cost about $12 billion when completed, nearly five times more than the $2.6 billion projected in 1985.[17] Road finances have also suffered from poor forecasts of demand. One study

16. This figure is based on estimates in Fedral Highway Administration, *Nationwide Personal Transportation Survey*, and the Bureau of the Census *Journey to Work Survey*.
17. General Accounting Office, *Transportation Infrastructure: Progress on and Challenges to Central Artery/Tunnel Project's Costs and Financing*, GAO/RCED-97-170 (July 1997).

found that ten of fourteen toll road projects experienced toll revenues in their first four years well below projections.[18] Finally, highway demonstration or pork barrel projects—the Transportation Equity Act contains some $9 billion of these—has increased the nation's highway bill.

The motoring public has become frustrated with road construction because it has not prevented urban automobile congestion from increasing.[19] Vehicle-miles traveled in urban areas increased 70 percent from 1980 to 1994, while urban road mileage increased only 30 percent.[20] The portion of urban highways with peak-hour traffic volume exceeding 71 percent of design capacity, a common indicator of congestion, increased steadily during the 1980s, occurring on over 50 percent of urban interstate miles and 40 percent of other freeway miles (figure 1-3). Although workplace and residential adjustments during the 1990s, such as working and living in outlying suburbs, have helped stabilize the extent of urban congestion, the current annual costs to travelers, mainly in the form of wasted time but also extra consumption of gasoline and vehicle wear and tear, have been estimated to run as high as $40 billion. And the annual cost of congestion to shippers, in the form of higher inventories and more goods stuck in transit, adds considerably to this figure.[21]

Highway construction has often been slowed because some neighborhoods (in Boston and San Francisco, for example) resist demolitions for expressways that will mostly serve suburban commuting to downtown. Of course, some suburban communities see little reason to support transit systems for central city neighborhoods. The result is that public officials are

18. Robert H. Muller, "Examining Toll Road Feasibility Studies," *Public Works Financing* (June 1996), pp. 16–20.

19. For a comprehensive discussion of congestion see Anthony Downs, *Stuck in Traffic: Coping with Peak-Hour Traffic Congestion* (Brookings, 1992). Roads have also suffered from pavement damage caused by heavy trucks. For a discussion of this problem and a proposed solution see Kenneth A. Small, Clifford Winston, and Carol A. Evans, *Road Work: A New Highway Pricing and Investment Policy* (Brookings, 1989).

20. These figures are from the Federal Highway Administration, *Highway Statistics*, (various years), tables HM-18 and VM-1.

21. Estimates of the costs of automobile congestion to travelers are produced by the Texas Transportation Institute at Texas A&M University. Thomas Corsi and others, *Transportation Study 1997*, report 3 (Washington: Greater Washington Board of Trade, April 1997), estimate that congestion raises the Washington area's annual freight bill alone by nearly $350 million. The increased cost to the nation's freight bill from congestion is substantially higher.

Figure 1-3. *Road Miles at More than 71 Percent Capacity during Peak Hours, 1980–94*

Percent

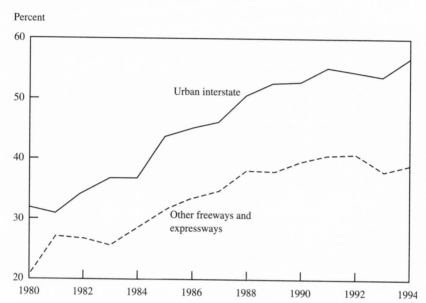

Source: Federal Highway Administration, *Highway Statistics* (Department of Transportation, annual), table HM-61.

often characterized as struggling to achieve some sort of balance between automobiles and transit.

Other Auto and Transit Issues

Concerns about urban transportation in the United States go beyond cost and service quality. Vehicle pollution, safety, and accessibility to jobs and recreational activities are also important considerations. Emissions from cars, buses, and trucks typically account for a large part of three major air pollutants—carbon monoxide, volatile organic compounds, and nitrogen oxides. Air quality in the United States has improved steadily since the 1960s, largely because of improvements in automobile emissions controls, but there has been less improvement in the urban concentration of ozone, for which motor vehicles bear substantial responsibility. Recent empirical

studies find that the health costs from local air pollution caused by the automobile run as high as $0.03 per vehicle mile in certain areas. Costs of bus
emissions, which include diesel particulates, are even higher.[22]

Although the motor vehicle fatality rate has sharply declined during the
past ten years, partly because of the greater use of seat belts, the widespread
introduction of air bags, and increased efforts to curb drunk driving, motor
vehicle accidents are still the ninth leading cause of death in the United
States. The annual cost of automobile accidents was estimated at $333 bil-
lion in 1988, or $0.164 per vehicle mile.[23] Although the annual costs from
bus and rail accidents are not nearly as large, transit's safety record calculated on the basis of passenger miles is roughly the same order of magnitude as that of the auto.[24]

A well-functioning urban transportation system can increase society's
productivity and welfare by improving people's access to jobs and recreational activities. The growth of jobs in the suburbs has been facilitated by
well-developed road systems and high rates of auto ownership. But people
who do not have ready access to cars cannot take advantage of suburban
jobs unless other forms of transportation serve the suburbs. Senior citizens
and young people who do not have ready access to cars may also be dependent on other forms of transportation if they wish to pursue certain recreational activities. As businesses and wealthier individuals leave the city for
the suburbs, and as unemployment rates in the inner cities rise relative to
rates in the suburbs, concern is mounting that our cities are in decline.
Improving urban transportation systems is seen by some as an important
step in reversing this decline.

22. This estimate was obtained for the Los Angeles region by Kenneth A. Small and Camilla
Kazimi, "On the Costs of Air Pollution from Motor Vehicles," *Journal of Transport Economics and
Policy*, vol. 29 (January 1995), pp. 7–32. The estimate is higher than estimates for average U.S.
metropolitan areas as reviewed by Kenneth A. Small, "Transportation and the Environment," in
R. Thord, ed., *The Future of Transportation and Communication* (Borlange: Swedish National
Road Administration, 1991), pp. 217–30.

23. See Ted R. Miller, "Costs and Functional Consequences of U.S. Roadway Crashes,"
Accident Analysis and Prevention, vol. 25 (1993), pp. 593–607.

24. The National Safety Council reports that during 1988–90 there were 1.12 automobile deaths
per 100 million passenger miles. APTA, *1992 Transit Fact Book*, p. 22. Data compiled from 1990
Urban Mass Transit Administration safety reports shows there were 1.01 rail deaths per 100 million passenger miles and 0.59 bus deaths per 100 million passenger miles.

Proposed Solutions

A casual reading of the op-ed page of most major newspapers suggests that urban transportation policymakers do not have to depend on Ph.D. qualifying examinations for proposed "solutions" to urban transportation problems. However, most solutions, whether from concerned citizens or the research community, mainly focus on highway congestion and take one of three approaches: increasing transportation capacity, managing existing capacity, or using prices to allocate scarce capacity.[25]

Those who advocate increasing transportation capacity believe that congestion can be relieved by building more roads and by adopting intelligent transportation systems (ITS) to alert travelers to alternative routes. They also believe that technologically advanced and efficient rail systems can attract substantially more people to mass transit and help relieve road congestion.[26]

Measures to manage existing transportation capacity are primarily designed to discourage peak-period highway use. These measures include high-occupancy vehicle (HOV) restrictions, exclusive bus lanes, and employer-based policies such as encouraging flexible work hours, eliminating free parking, and allowing telecommuting.[27]

Economists call for policymakers to replicate efficient market outcomes by setting *efficient prices and service levels* for all transportation modes to best allocate scarce urban transportation resources. Some economists argue that the public sector will never promote efficiency in urban transportation but that these services can become more efficient if they are privatized.[28]

---

25. Efforts to improve urban transportation by altering land use policies are considered to have little effect. See Don Pickrell, "Transportation and Land Use," in Gomez-Ibañez, Tye, and Winston, eds., *Essays in Transportation Economics and Policy*.

26. See John F. Kain, "How to Improve Urban Transportation at Practically No Cost," *Public Policy*, vol. 20 (Summer 1972), pp. 335–58.

27. See Kenneth A. Small and José A. Gomez-Ibañez, "Urban Transportation," in Paul Cheshire and Edwin S. Mills, eds., *Handbook of Regional and Urban Economics,* vol. 3: *Applied Urban Economics* (Amsterdam: North-Holland, forthcoming), for a full discussion of congestion or transportation demand management.

28. For discussions of privatization see Lave, ed., *Urban Transit*; Robert W. Poole Jr., and Philip E. Fixler Jr., "Privatization of Public-Sector Services in Practice: Experience and Potential," *Journal of Policy Analysis and Management*, vol. 6 (Summer 1987), pp. 612–25; José A. Gomez-Ibañez and John R. Meyer, *Going Private: The International Experience with Transport Privatization* (Brookings, 1993); and Gabriel Roth, *Roads in a Market Economy* (Aldershot, England: Avebury Technical, 1996).

So far, attempts to reduce congestion by increasing capacity or managing existing capacity more effectively have not met with great success. Additional rail systems and more roads have not reduced congestion because commuters have shifted from less preferred modes of travel and times of day to fill peak-period highway capacity.[29] It is also unlikely that expensive intelligent transportation systems, which provide up-to-date traffic information to drivers, would have a significant effect on congestion because all motorists would have access to the same information and would converge on the least congested routes.[30] Thus these systems may not be justifiable on cost-benefit grounds. Several studies have found that transportation demand management programs have proven very costly and had little effect on travel behavior.[31] A few policies such as exclusive bus lanes and ramp metering may be cost effective but provide only a little relief from congestion.

Economic approaches have received little attention from policymakers, possibly because little is known about how an economically efficient urban transportation policy would actually work or because economists' enthusiasm for efficient prices—which in practice means *higher* prices for auto users—may elicit strong objections from travelers and policymakers.[32]

This book is an attempt to present a comprehensive solution to urban transportation problems that is both informed by decades of economic

29. This idea is known as Downs's law: on urban commuter expressways, peak-hour traffic congestion increases to meet maximum capacity because commuters shift from less preferred modes and times of day. Anthony Downs, "The Law of Peak-Hour Expressway Congestion," *Traffic Quarterly,* vol. 16 (July 1962), pp. 393–409.

30. Clifford Winston, "Building a Better Traffic Jam," *New York Times*, December 21, 1991, p. A 19, argues that Downs's law will still apply if intelligent transportation systems (ITS) are introduced.

31. See, for example, David Brownstone and Thomas F. Golob, "The Effectiveness of Ridesharing Incentives: Discrete-Choice Models of Commuting in Southern California," *Regional Science and Urban Economics*, vol. 22 (March 1992), pp. 5–24; Genevieve Giuliano, "Transportation Demand Management: Promise or Panacea?" *Journal of the American Planning Association*, vol. 58 (Summer 1992), pp. 327–35; and Apogee Research, *Costs and Effectiveness of Transportation Control Measures (TCMs): A Review and Analysis of the Literature* (Washington: National Association of Regional Councils, 1994).

32. Policymakers have expressed some interest in congestion pricing experiments. But the major experiment on the San Francisco Bay Bridge that had been authorized by Congress failed to be implemented; see Stephen Shmanske, "The Bay Bridge Blunder," *Regulation*, Vol. 19, no. 4 (1996), pp. 58–64.

research and cognizant of the political constraints on policymakers that can relegate economists' solutions to collecting dust on bookshelves. We first look at the magnitude of current inefficiencies by estimating the social benefits to the United States from a package of efficient pricing and service policies for the major urban transportation modes and find that this policy could generate considerably more than $10 billion (1990 dollars) in annual net benefits over current practice. The sources of these benefits indicate that current urban transit subsidies cannot be justified on the grounds that auto travel is underpriced. Keeping in mind that this is a conservative estimate, it seems large enough to arouse interest. We then identify the political and institutional sources of the current inefficiencies and assess whether it is possible for urban transportation to become significantly more efficient while the public sector is responsible for its provision. Our findings suggest that government subsidies, the influence of various transportation constituencies, and institutional decision structures that allow public officials to pursue objectives inconsistent with economic efficiency account for most of the deviations from an efficient policy. These political forces are sufficiently powerful to prevent society from realizing the benefits of a more efficient public urban transportation system, so that it is fruitless for economists to continue to advocate efficient solutions to improve these systems.

Economic research, however, has helped influence policymakers to replace government regulation with unregulated competition in several U.S. industries, which has substantially improved resource allocation in the United States.[33] We therefore consider whether the private sector could significantly improve the U.S. urban transportation system. We believe it could. In fact, we find that some form of privatization of urban transportation could improve social welfare by as much as, if not more than, an efficient public sector system. Facing fewer operating restrictions, greater economic incentives, and stronger competitive pressures, private suppliers of urban transportation could significantly improve the efficiency of urban operations and offer services that are more responsive to the preferences of all travelers. Moreover, these improvements are not likely to come at the

---

33. Clifford Winston, "U.S. Industry Adjustment to Economic Deregulation," *Journal of Economic Perspectives*, vol. 12 (Summer 1998).

expense of a massive redistribution of income from economically disadvantaged travelers to wealthier citizens and operators.

Policymakers have bestowed huge benefits on the public by allowing the private sector to take an unencumbered lead in providing intercity transportation.[34] The public will be similarly rewarded if they take the next step and allow the private sector to play a leading role in providing urban transportation.

34. Steven A. Morrison and Clifford Winston, "Regulatory Reform of U.S. Intercity Transportation," in Gomez-Ibañez, Tye, and Winston, eds., *Essays in Transportation Economics and Policy.*

2

The Urban Transit Operating and Institutional Environment

TRANSIT SYSTEMS are a varied lot: old and new, large and small, public and private. The oldest street railway line still in operation is the New Orleans and Carrollton line, formed in 1835. The newest transit system is Dallas's light rail system, which started running in June 1996. New York City's transit system, the country's largest, carries some 2 billion rail and bus passengers a year and covers 2,300 rail and bus route miles. The smallest system, the Benton Harbor–Twin Cities transit system in Michigan, carries only 34,000 passengers a year over 16 route miles.[1] Most transit systems are public. Some cities give private bus companies operating rights, although *none* of these private companies makes fare and route decisions on its own. (Private systems also usually receive financial assistance from local governments.) Fares and routes are determined in all cases by a local or state authority, although private companies can offer advice. Paratransit operations, which are largely but not exclusively private, fall between the private automobile and conventional bus and include jitneys, commuter vans, employer shuttles, demand-responsive systems, and so on.[2]

Detailed discussions of urban transit systems and the policymaking bodies responsible for regulating their operations can be found in several sources.[3] A summary of the most prominent features of these systems and

---

1. Department of Transportation, 1994 Section 15 database.
2. See Robert Cervero, *Paratransit in America: Redefining Mass Transportation* (Praeger, 1997).
3. See, for example, Gordon J. Fielding, *Managing Public Transit Strategically: A Comprehensive Approach to Strengthening Service and Monitoring Performance* (San Francisco: Jossey-Bass, 1987); and American Public Transit Association (APTA), *Transit Fact Book* (Washington, annual).

the relevant kinds of policymakers provides a useful context for understanding the sources of current inefficiencies.

Operating Characteristics

The U.S. Department of Transportation collects data on transit systems for urbanized areas, called UZAs.[4] Our empirical analysis will focus on systems in urban areas with populations of at least 200,000, the largest 116 UZAs in the country. The Department of Transportation classifies transit systems as bus, rapid rail, light rail, or trolley bus. We classify rapid rail, light rail, and trolley bus as rail systems and treat them homogeneously because they all depend on fixed guideways. The operating characteristics of the 228 bus operations and 30 rail operations in these UZAs are presented in table 2-1. The average rail operation covers one-tenth the route miles of the average bus operation but provides seven times the vehicle capacity, as measured in seat miles, three times the vehicle miles, and carries four times the passengers. Rail operating revenues and expenses are, on average, more than four times those of bus systems.[5]

The differences between bus and rail operations have significant economic implications. Because rail runs more frequently than bus over a smaller route network and generally carries more passenger miles per vehicle mile (see table 2-1), the average rail operation is able to realize more economies of route density and vehicle size. These economies help keep rail operating expenses per passenger mile lower than those of the average bus operation and help keep its average farebox recovery (the difference between its revenues and operating expenses) higher than that

4. For convenience, a particular geographical area is often referred to by its major city. A city, however, is actually defined by its political boundaries. An MSA, or metropolitan statistical area, is a federal government definition of a geographical area that is typically larger than the immediate city. An urbanized area, UZA, is a Department of Transportation definition. Its geographical coverage strongly overlaps with an MSA. It also excludes rural areas, which is appropriate for this analysis.

5. New York City transit companies constitute a large part of the transit operations that are conducted in this country. If these companies are excluded from our comparison, rail revenues and costs are, on average, about two and a half times greater than those of bus.

Table 2-1. *Operating Characteristics of Bus and Rail Transit Companies, 1990*

Characteristic	Bus	Rail
Number of companies in sample	228	30
Service indicators		
Average route miles	637.0	61.1
Average annual seat miles (millions)	386.9	2,520.1
Average annual vehicle revenue miles (millions)[a]	5.8	18.6
Average passengers (millions)	20.0	88.2
Financial indicators		
Average passenger revenues (millions of dollars)	12.4	62.1
Average operating expense (millions of dollars)	32.2	139.0
Hourly vehicle revenue miles per route mile[a]	1.0	17.0
Passenger miles per vehicle revenue mile[a]	9.0	21.0
Operating expense per passenger mile (cents)	44.0	37.0
Passenger revenue per operating expense (percent)	33.8	39.3

Sources: Federal Transit Administration, data tables for the 1990 Section 15 database; and authors' calculations.

a. Vehicle revenue miles are vehicle miles that could generate revenue to a transit company. In most discussions the term is shortened to vehicle miles.

of the average bus operation.[6] Rail systems may appear to be more efficient than bus systems because rail operations are on average located in more densely populated areas. If bus operations were limited to corridors with high traffic density, or if bus companies had the incentive and flexibility to adjust their vehicle sizes, bus costs would probably be lower than rail costs.[7]

All rail systems are publicly owned, as are the vast majority of bus systems (some 90 percent of vehicle miles). The remaining bus systems are private (6 percent of vehicle miles) or contracted to serve a city (4 percent

6. Joseph Berechman, *Public Transit Economics and Deregulation Policy* (Amsterdam:North-Holland, 1993), finds bus companies show only modest economies of scale, but Berechman and Philip A. Viton, "Consolidations of Scale and Scope in Urban Transit," *Regional Science and Urban Economics*, vol. 22 (March 1992), pp. 25–49, find rail companies exhibit economies of scale and traffic density.

7. For example, Theodore E. Keeler, Kenneth A. Small, and associates, *The Full Costs of Urban Transport,* Part III: *Automobile Costs and Final Intermodal Cost Comparisons,* monograph 21 (Institute of Urban and Regional Development, University of California, Berkeley, 1975), find that San Francisco Bay Area bus operations have lower costs per passenger trip than Bay Area Rapid Transit (BART) operations for comparable passenger levels.

Table 2-2. *Private and Public Bus Operations, 1990*[a]

Characteristic	Private	Comparable public
Financial indicators		
Average fare (cents per trip)	56.7	41.1
Operating expense per seat mile (cents per mile)	5.1	5.3
Operating expense per passenger mile (cents per mile)	35.0	42.9
Passenger revenue per operating expense (percent)	51.8	27.6
Service indicators		
Frequency (vehicle miles per route mile per hour)	1.1	0.8
Route coverage (miles/square miles)	1.18	2.51

Sources: Federal Transit Administration, data tables for the 1990 Section 15 database; and authors' calculations.

a. Cities with only private bus operations are Las Vegas; New Haven; Charleston, S.C.; and Columbia, S.C. Comparable cities with populations between 325,000 and 700,000 and with only public bus operations (no private or purchased transportation) are Birmingham, Ala.; Honolulu; Rochester, N.Y.; Dayton; Richmond, Va.; Tucson; Nashville, Tenn.; El Paso; Omaha; Akron; Albany; Albuquerque; Toledo; Oxnard; Tulsa; Fresno; Wilmington; Grand Rapids, Mich.; Bridgeport; Baton Rouge; Youngstown; Colorado Springs; Wichita; and Flint.

of vehicle miles).[8] (Public paratransit systems account for a very small share of trips.) Although private operations are not completely free to make fare and route decisions on their own, they have more flexibility than public systems to improve the efficiency of their operations. Table 2-2 compares the operating characteristics of certain private and public bus companies. The private companies operate in four cities that are served only by private bus, thus preventing the comparison from being biased, as it would have been had we included companies that operate on only the most profitable routes in the city and leave unprofitable routes for public bus operations.[9] The control group of public bus companies serves twenty-four cities ranging in size between the smallest and largest of the four cities with pri-

8. These figures are from the Department of Transportation, 1990 Section 15 database. Private systems are privately owned; contract services may be provided by public agencies or private carriers. Roger F. Teal, "Public Transit Service Contracting: A Status Report," *Transportation Quarterly*, vol. 42 (April 1988), pp. 207–22, and José A. Gomez-Ibañez and John R. Meyer, *Going Private: The International Experience with Transport Privatization* (Brookings, 1993), report that contracting for transit service has been increasing slowly since the 1980s. Similarly, Philip A. Viton, "Private Roads," *Journal of Urban Economics,* vol. 37 (May 1995), pp. 260–89, notes that there is growing interest in private sector involvement in the provision of highways.

9. These systems receive subsidies that, on average, are lower than subsidies to public systems. Because the private systems are not completely free to make fare and route decisions, this comparison is likely to understate the benefits of flexibility.

vate systems.[10] As the table shows, private companies on average set higher fares and operate with lower expenses than public companies, which enables them to service a city with much lower subsidies than a public system.[11] Private bus companies' operating cost advantage over public companies appears to derive from more frequent service over a smaller route network and lower wages and less restrictive work rules.[12] We will return to this finding in chapter 6 when we argue that the benefits of a privatized bus industry partly derive from its freedom to realize greater cost efficiencies in network design and from its ability to reduce labor costs and make more efficient use of capital, labor, and fuel.

A Brief Comparison with Auto Costs

Transit systems are able to reduce the costs of a passenger mile when their vehicles run frequently *and* are filled with paying passengers, that is, they achieve high load factors. In principle, the economies from larger vehicle sizes give transit a cost advantage over automobiles. In urbanized areas, rail's 5.8 cents average operating cost per seat mile and bus's 5.9 cents are lower than auto's 7.8 cents.[13] But this potential cost advantage is not realized in practice because bus and rail typically operate with a great deal of excess capacity. In our sample, rail's average load factor is

10. There may be differences between cities that have private bus companies and those that do not that affect bus costs, but it is difficult to control for these differences in this simple comparison.

11. Paul N. Tramontozzi and Kenneth W. Chilton, *The Federal Free Ride: The Economics and Politics of U.S. Transit Policy* (Center for the Study of American Business, Washington University, 1987), find that private systems have succeeded in providing 20 to 50 percent more service per dollar of cost than public systems. Indeed, officials in Falls Church, Virginia, have claimed that a private contractor could provide comparable service at 60 percent less than Metro, the Washington, D.C., area system, costs the city. Falls Church agreed to stay with Metrorail after the Northern Virginia Transportation Commission agreed to cover the difference in cost for two years. See Alice Reid, "Metrobus's Future is Topic of Summit," *Washington Post,* January 5, 1997, p. B4.

12. Alice Reid, "Bumpy Road Ahead for Metrobus Plan," *Washington Post*, August 24, 1997, p. B1, reports that the typical Metrobus driver gets paid as much as 50 percent more than drivers for private bus companies in the Washington area.

13. The figures for bus and rail are calculated from the Department of Transportation, 1990 Section 15 database, and the figure for automobiles, which assumes an average seating capacity of four people, is from Runzheimer International, Rochester, Wisc.

17.6 percent and bus's is 14.3 percent.[14] Auto's average load factor, based on an average vehicle occupancy of 1.5 people and an average vehicle capacity of 4 people, is 37.5 percent. Thus, auto's 21 cents average operating cost per passenger mile is considerably below rail's 37 cents and bus's 44 cents.[15] As we show later, the difference between auto and transit costs per passenger mile is hardly affected when we account for pollution and other social costs.

This comparison reveals another inefficiency in transit operations—excess capacity, which, as illustrated by deregulated intercity transportation carriers, could be reduced with some fundamental changes in operating practices. Railroads and trucking companies have become more responsive to shippers and have virtually eliminated empty return hauls. Airlines use larger aircraft on long-haul routes and smaller ones on short-haul routes because their traffic density generally increases with distance. Intercity bus companies have developed van systems to serve rural communities. In principle, transit companies could reduce excess capacity by becoming better informed about and more responsive to travelers' schedules and by adjusting their vehicle sizes. But unlike deregulated intercity transportation firms, public transit companies appear to lack the flexibility and incentive to take these steps.

Institutional Environment

The major economic decisions a transit system faces are what fares to charge, what routes to cover and how often to cover them, and where to spend federal grant money. For a given transit system these decisions are made, in principle, by a state, county, or city policymaking body. Complications can arise, however, when trying to identify the actual decisionmaker because other individuals or groups can exert a subtle influence. For example, a transit authority may have the power to set fares in a given urban area, but the governor may influence the authority board's decisions

14. Transit's average load factor has been declining for some time. It was 22 percent in 1975, it was 18 percent in 1985, and 16 percent in 1995.

15. These figures are also from the Department of Transportation Section 15 database and Runzheimer International.

Table 2-3. *Controlling Entity for Transit Operations and Federal Grant Money in Cities Surveyed, 1990*

Number of cities

Controlling entity	Final say over mass transit route selection	Final say over mass transit fare decisions	Direct recipient of federal grant money for mass transit
State	3	3	29
State department of transportation[a]	2	. . .	40
County	3	6	8
City	18	20	20
Metropolitan planning organization	10	3	3
Transit authority	80	81	16
Elected	2	2	0
Appointed by governor	16	18	3
Appointed by city council or mayor	39	37	8
Appointed by other[b]	23	24	5

Source: Authors' survey in conjunction with the National Association of Regional Councils.
a. In the case of direct recipient of federal grant money, entity is a special district rather than a state department of transportation.
b. Includes multiple entities, the county, metropolitan planning organization, or the transit company.

because he or she appoints the board members. In addition, a policymaking body may be more influential if it has an independent source of funds. We therefore conducted a survey that identified the designated decisionmakers for the transit systems in our sample and identified any possible external influences on their decisions.[16]

Table 2-3 summarizes which decisionmakers make which decisions in our sample.[17] Power to set fares and determine route coverage usually belongs to transit authorities, which are composed of board members that are usually appointed by state or local officials. Most cities lacking a transit authority rely on a local entity, either a city official such as a mayor or a metropolitan planning organization (MPO), for decisionmaking.[18] Less than 10 percent of the cities leave these decisions to the governor, state

16. We are grateful to the National Association of Regional Councils for their assistance in preparing and executing the survey and in obtaining the full cooperation of the transportation decisionmakers for the urbanized areas in our sample.

17. There does not seem to be a systematic explanation for why certain entities are responsible for these decisions or why a particular entity bears responsibility for these decisions in a given urbanized area. In most cases the decisionmaker appears to be determined by historical precedent.

18. An MPO is similar to a transit authority but is concerned with a broader range of transportation issues, such as intermodal coordination and highway investments.

department of transportation, or county.[19] But in a quarter of the cities in our sample, governors can influence fare and route decisions because they appoint the members of the transit authority or MPO. Mayors and city councils can also have more influence on fare and route decisions than is indicated in table 2-3 because they each appoint transit authority members in about 25 percent of the cities. In the remaining cities, members were either elected, appointed by the MPO or county, or, in Baton Rouge, appointed by the head of the transit company.

Federal money earmarked for urban transit does not go directly to the companies in a transit system but to one of the local or state entities listed in table 2-3. Not surprisingly, the recipient of the federal grant money for mass transit can influence the way it is spent. The most frequent recipients of these funds are special transportation districts, followed by the states.[20] Other city and county entities also receive federal money, depending on the city. [21]

Conclusion

In this chapter, we have suggested that transit's economic efficiency is being compromised by public sector decisionmakers. Accordingly, it is possible that some of them are more likely than others to promote or discourage urban transit efficiency. We will investigate this issue after characterizing the features of an efficient public urban transportation system.

19. Governors are much more important factors in the selection of highway projects.

20. A special district is a single-purpose level of government that consists of a tailored geographical area. A special district can submit grant proposals to the federal government, in which case it would be the direct recipient of federal money for transit.

21. For highways the state is almost always the recipient of the federal grant money.

3

Travelers' Preferences for Urban Transportation

THE U.S. URBAN transportation system is characterized by large public transit deficits and severe highway congestion. One source of the deficits appears to be inefficient operations. Another may be that transit policymakers set inefficient prices and service levels, which generate less revenue than is warranted for the service provided. Inefficient pricing of automobile travel, which makes it less costly than its impact on other drivers would warrant, could be responsible for severe highway congestion.

Economic theory suggests that urban transportation pricing and service inefficiencies could be ameliorated if travelers were charged for the marginal cost of their trips and if service were provided to the point where the marginal benefit from additional service were equal to its marginal cost. Analyzing the economic effects of this policy requires an understanding of travelers' preferences for urban transportation and how their welfare will be affected by changes in transportation prices and service. In this chapter we develop a model of travelers' choices of mode and departure time that will provide this understanding.

Modeling Travel Decisions

Travelers' short-term responses to changes in the price and service of urban transportation can take any of five general forms. For example, in response to a new peak-period highway toll, some auto travelers might simply pay the toll and not adjust their travel behavior; others might try to avoid the increased expense by switching to transit (*mode shift*), commuting during an off-peak period (*departure-time shift*), traveling on nontoll local roads (*route shift*), or changing the number of trips they take (*trip generation*). In the long run they might travel to different destinations and even change their residential location.

We use an urban travel demand model of mode and departure-time choice to capture the first three of the five potential short-run responses.[1] We could crudely model changes in route choice as well, but we believe that the effect of this response on travelers' welfare is likely to be small.[2] We are not able to model how changes in an urban transportation system explicitly affect the number of trips travelers make, but we can assess the effect of this restriction on our findings. Finally, we are not able to model changes in travelers' destinations or residential locations, but again we can assess how our findings would be affected if we could account for these long-term responses.

An Aggregate Joint-Choice Model

Most contemporary analyses of urban travel behavior take a disaggregate modeling approach, which requires data for each traveler's mode choice for work or pleasure trips, fares and service characteristics for the modes that, in principle, could provide these trips, and each traveler's socioeconomic characteristics. These data are then used to estimate the effect of modal attributes and travelers' socioeconomic characteristics on mode choices. Because we were interested in analyzing urban travel behavior throughout the country, not in just one or a few cities, a fully disaggregate approach to our problem would have imposed excessive data collection and estimation requirements.

As an alternative approach, we developed an aggregate model of traveler behavior in which we combined mode and departure-time choices by distance of commute for a large cross section of urban areas in the United States. We will validate this approach by comparing some of our most important estimation results with those based on models estimated with

1. Urban travel demand models have a long history in transportation economics. Kenneth A. Small, *Urban Transportation Economics* (Philadelphia: Harwood Academic Publishers, 1992), provides an extensive review of them.

2. In some urban areas (for example, ones with major corridors that are connected by bridges or tunnels), travelers do not have a choice among alternative routes, especially for work trips. In addition, to the extent that alternative routes are available, it is likely that their characteristics will also be affected by a change in transportation prices or service.

fully disaggregated data. We will also discuss how the limitations imposed by not using fully disaggregated data are likely to affect our characterization of the economic effects of an efficient urban transportation policy.

In our analysis, travelers are assumed to select the travel mode and departure time that *jointly* maximizes their utility (for example, a utility-maximizing choice could consist of departing between 8:00 a.m. and 8:30 a.m. and traveling by automobile). We will determine the variables that influence this joint choice and demonstrate the plausibility of the estimated parameters by using them to estimate travelers' value of time and the net benefits travelers attach to each urban transportation mode.

Construction of the Sample

The 1990 Census of Population and Housing collected data on individual commuters' journey to work, including their choice of mode and departure time. Because travelers' valuations of modal attributes may be affected by the length of their commute, we obtained from the Census Bureau a version of the sample in which travelers' choices of mode and departure time for each urban area were disaggregated into five commute distances: 0 miles to less than 1 mile, 1–5 miles, 6–10 miles, 11–25 miles, and greater than 25 miles.[3] We used this sample to estimate joint choice models by these distances based on travel behavior in the largest 116 urbanized areas in the country.

By using such commute distance blocks we captured some of the spatial dimension of commuting. For example, commutes of less than 1 mile are likely to be within the central business district, commutes greater than 25 miles are likely to be from suburban residences to the central business districts, or possibly from suburban residences to suburban workplaces, and so on.[4] One deficiency of these data is that they only include work trips, which in 1990 accounted for roughly 20 percent of all urban trips. But by making plausible assumptions about the relationship

3. We are grateful to Don Dalzell of the Census Bureau for making the data available to us by commute distance block.

4. Estimating a joint-choice model based on spatial classifications (for example, combining all commutes from the suburbs to the central business district) instead of well-defined commute distance blocks was not likely to improve our analysis and could have led to greater aggregation problems because we would have been forced to combine trips of vastly different distances.

between work trip and non–work trip behavior, and subjecting these assumptions to sensitivity analysis, we can extrapolate our findings from work trips to all trips.

For each commute distance block, we computed an average commute distance as a weighted average of the actual commute distances within that block.[5] We assumed that, for a given average distance, travelers choose among five modes and ten departure-time blocks. The modes included single-occupant vehicle (automobile), multi-occupant vehicle (carpool, vanpool), bus, rail, and taxi.[6] The ten departure-time blocks included a large 12:00 a.m.–5:00 a.m. block encompassing the hours before normal commute times, then eight half-hour blocks for the 5:00 a.m.–9:00 a.m. morning commute, and an hour block, 9:00 a.m.–10:00 a.m., at the end of the morning commute.[7] Thus, travelers' choice sets are composed of fifty combinations of mode and departure time. The purpose of our demand model was to explain, for a given average commute distance, the *share* of travel on a given mode during a given departure-time block.

Explanatory Variables

We assumed choices of mode and departure time in an urbanized area to be influenced by the attributes of the travel modes, departure-time characteristics, and socioeconomic characteristics of the area. The modal attributes we included are fares, route coverage, frequency of service, and travel time. The use of aggregate data raises some questions about the way these variables should be constructed. We generally found, however, that our results were not particularly sensitive to the approach we took.

Fares were calculated for all modes for each average commute distance. Most transit systems charge fares that are constant for most trip

5. The average commute distances by distance block are 0.5 miles, 3 miles, 7.5 miles, 15 miles, and 45 miles.

6. Systems with fixed guideways—light rail, heavy rail, and trolleybus—are included in the rail alternative. Commuters do rely on bicycle, ferry service, and other modes of transportation besides those listed, but these modes have a tiny share of the travel market.

7. We specified other departure-time blocks, such as those after 10:00 a.m., and blocks during the morning rush hour that were as narrow as fifteen minutes, but these alternative specifications did not have much effect on our findings.

distances, so for bus and rail we calculated uniform fares equal to passenger revenues divided by passenger trips.[8] We then performed sensitivity analyses in which we increased these fares during the peak travel period and for longer-distance commutes, but we found that our results were not affected by these modifications, so we used the uniform fares in our model.[9] Auto fares (costs) include the full operating costs per mile of driving to work.[10] Carpool costs were obtained by dividing the single-occupant automobile costs by the national weighted average of the number of riders in a carpool.[11] Finally, taxi fares are based on one passenger per cab and include a cost for the first mile, additional mileage costs, and a 15 percent tip for the driver.[12] We expected an increase in fares to decrease the likelihood that a given mode and departure time would be selected.

We calculated in-vehicle travel time for each departure time period by dividing the average commute distance by a mode's average speed. In the case of transit, we added waiting time to in-vehicle time to obtain total travel time.[13] The average speeds for bus and rail were obtained by dividing vehicle miles by their vehicle hours. Because a bus's average speed could vary by time of day or even by the distance of the commute, we reduced bus speeds during peak travel periods and increased them for longer commutes. But

8. Passenger revenue and passenger trips were obtained from the Department of Transportation Section 15 database.

9. We also calculated bus and rail fares per mile and estimated models with these fares instead of uniform fares. Although this construction of transit fares did not lead to any significant changes in our findings, the models of choice that were estimated with them produced less satisfactory statistical fits than models estimated with uniform fares.

10. These costs are from Runzheimer International. They include vehicle depreciation, which is appropriate because people purchase automobiles primarily for commuting to work.

11. We used the national average because we were not able to get the average number of riders in a carpool for a large segment of the urbanized areas in our sample. The number of riders in a carpool in a sample of forty urbanized areas ranged from 2.2 to 2.5. The figure we used is 2.5, based on the national average of riders in a carpool according to the Federal Highway Administration, 1983 *Nationwide Personal Transportation Survey* (Department of Transportation).

12. These fares were obtained from a Brookings Institution survey of taxi commissions in the urbanized areas in our sample.

13. The census data include travel times for all modes. But we obtained more satisfactory statistical fits and were able to vary highway travel times in accordance with the level of congestion by using the travel times constructed here.

because these modifications did not affect our findings, we did not include them in our model.[14] To measure waiting time for bus and rail service, we used the common rule of thumb that waiting time is half the headway (time between vehicles) up to a maximum of fifteen minutes.[15] The average speed for an automobile, including a taxi, was determined by the average speeds on local roads and highways, weighted by the mileage a commuter spends on these thoroughfares. Our procedure for calculating the average speeds and mileage a commuter spends on local roads and highways for an average commuting distance is presented in appendix A. These speeds will vary throughout the day in accordance with the density of traffic. To account for picking up and dropping off additional riders, we assumed that carpool travel times are five minutes longer than single-occupant vehicle times for average commutes less than ten miles. And following John Kain, we assumed that they are eight minutes longer than single-occupant vehicle travel times for average commutes greater than ten miles.[16] We expected an increase in travel time to decrease the likelihood that a given mode and departure time would be selected. We captured any unmeasured attributes of carpooling, such as reduced privacy, with a carpool dummy variable.[17]

Route coverage indicates the extent to which a mode provides accessibility to work and leisure activities in an urbanized area. It is defined for bus and rail as a system's route miles divided by the area of the urbanized area (UZA).

14. Bus and rail vehicle miles and hours were obtained from the Section 15 database. We adjusted bus speeds during peak and off-peak periods by scaling them in proportion to how auto speeds changed during these periods. The average speed for a bus in our sample is 13.5 miles per hour and the average speed for rail is 18.0 miles per hour.

15. According to tabulations of the Federal Highway Administration, *1990 Nationwide Personal Transportation Survey*, 52 percent of travelers wait less than five minutes for service, 21 percent wait five to ten minutes, 18 percent wait ten to twenty minutes, and 9 percent wait longer than twenty minutes. We also estimated models in which we assumed uniform waiting times of five minutes or no waiting time, in which case the full effect of waiting time was captured by service frequency. These estimations did not lead to any important changes in our findings. Finally, we do not attempt to explicitly account for access time here, but this effect is captured by route coverage.

16. John F. Kain, "Impacts of Congestion Pricing on Transit and Carpool Demand and Supply," in National Research Council, *Curbing Gridlock: Peak-Period Fees to Relieve Traffic Congestion*, vol. 2: *Commissioned Papers* (Washington: National Academy Press, 1994), p. 517.

17. We also specified a dummy variable in the carpool alternative that indicated whether an urbanized area had high occupancy vehicle (HOV) lanes, but this variable was statistically insignificant. Alternative-specific dummies for the other modes were also statistically insignificant.

Route coverage for auto, carpool, and taxi are defined as the miles of road in the UZA divided by its area.[18] Recall that UZAs do not include rural areas, which is appropriate for the construction of this variable. We expected an increase in route coverage to increase the likelihood of a given mode's being selected.

A mode's convenience to travelers is captured by its service frequency. Bus and rail service frequency is defined as daily vehicle revenue miles per route mile. Transit frequencies have been adjusted to account for their greater frequency during peak hours.[19] Because travelers generally do not have to use their cars according to a fixed schedule, auto frequency is, in principle, infinite. Nonetheless, a reasonable way to measure auto (and taxi) frequency, especially as it compares with transit frequency, is to divide daily vehicle miles by the road mileage of the UZA.[20] The frequency that is obtained is at least an order of magnitude greater than transit frequency. (Our findings were not affected when we estimated alternative specifications that allowed automobile and taxi frequency to be arbitrarily high.) We expect an increase in frequency to increase the likelihood that a given mode and departure time would be selected.

Finally, we included an urban area's average household income in the specification by dividing the average fare or cost and travel time by it.[21] We

18. Route miles for bus and rail systems are from the Department of Transportation Section 15 database. We were not able to determine whether route coverage varied between peak and off-peak periods. It is not likely, however, that many transit systems' route coverage varies significantly over the day. The road miles and areas of the UZAs in our sample are from the Federal Highway Administration, *Highway Statistics 1990,* table HM-71.

19. According to the Department of Transportation Section 15 database, the average peak-to-base ratios for rail and bus, where the peak period is 6:30–9:00 a.m., are 1.92 and 1.70, respectively. The peak-to-base ratio is the ratio of frequency during a peak hour to frequency during an average hour of the day. Transit frequencies could also vary by commute distance, but we were unable to verify this in a systematic fashion. Any marked difference in frequencies that did exist would, in all likelihood, lead to lower frequencies for long-distance trips. Because transit is already at a distinct disadvantage against the auto for these trips, it is unlikely that reducing transit frequencies for long-distance trips would have much effect on our findings.

20. Vehicle miles for bus and rail operations are obtained from the Department of Transportation Section 15 database. Automobile vehicle miles are from Federal Highway Administration, *Highway Statistics.*

21. We were unable to obtain data on an urban area's household income by commute distance block. Fred Mannering and Clifford Winston, "A Dynamic Empirical Analysis of Household Vehicle Ownership and Utilization," *Rand Journal of Economics,* vol. 16 (Summer 1985), pp. 215–36, used a specification of income that is similar to the one used here by dividing an automobile's price and operating cost by income. This specification imposes a restriction that the willingness to pay for, in our case, reductions in travel time is independent of income. This restriction, however, is not espe-

Table 3-1. *Means of Transportation Mode Attributes*

Attribute	Drive alone	Car pool	Bus	Rail	Taxi
Fare per mile (dollars)[a]	0.32	0.13	0.13	0.17	1.52
Route coverage (route or road miles per square mile of urbanized area)	9.74	9.74	2.59	0.10	9.74
Frequency (hourly vehicle miles per route or road miles), peak (6:30–9:00 a.m.)	209.4	209.4	1.6	38.7	209.4
Frequency (hourly vehicle miles per route or road miles), off-peak (times other than 6:30–9:00 a.m.)	209.4	209.4	0.9	20.8	209.4
In-vehicle time per mile (minutes per mile), peak (6:30–9:00 a.m.)	2.92	2.92	4.49	3.81	2.92
In-vehicle time per mile (minutes per mile), off-peak (times other than 6:30–9:00 a.m.)	2.58	2.58	4.49	3.81	2.58
Total travel time per mile (minutes per mile), peak (6:30–9:00 a.m.)[b]	2.92	4.47	8.56	4.95	2.92
Total travel time per mile (minutes per mile), off-peak (times other than 6:30–9:00 a.m.)[b]	2.58	4.12	8.95	5.74	2.58

Source: Authors' calculations. The means for the entire sample were obtained by taking a weighted average of the means for the commute distance blocks.

a. Transit fares are based on the uniform fare described in the text but are converted to dollars per mile.

b. Total travel time includes in-vehicle time and waiting time for bus and rail, and pickup and drop-off time for car pools.

also specified levels of car ownership and other socioeconomic variables, but they were statistically insignificant.[22]

The sample means of the modal attributes are presented in table 3-1. As expected, the automobile's advantage over transit lies in its service characteristics. Cars offer commuters greater speed, accessibility, and convenience during peak and off-peak periods. And transit's price advantage can be overcome by carpooling. The service advantage of automobiles takes on greater importance for long-distance, suburban-based commutes than for short commutes within central cities. We suggested earlier that

---

cially important to our analysis and does not affect our central findings. Moreover, we obtained the best statistical fits with this functional specification of income.

22. The small variation in auto ownership in our cross section of urban areas contributed to its lack of statistical significance.

current urban transportation policy has promoted inefficient operations and may also be promoting inefficient prices and service. A policy that seeks to maximize efficiency could therefore dramatically alter these attributes.

Departure times are determined by travelers' work schedules and the industry and regional influences that modify these schedules. Our joint-choice model thus includes dummies for departure-time preference for each time period except 12 a.m.–5 a.m., which serves as the base period. We also specified for each urbanized area the percentage of employment in the financial, real estate, and insurance sector as a percentage of total employment, interacted with departure times between 8 a.m. and 10 a.m., to account for the fact that people in these occupations tend to begin work later in the morning than people in other occupations. Finally, we indicated the number of hours that each urbanized area is behind eastern standard time (Los Angeles receives a value of three) to control for the possibility that people in later time zones have a preference for earlier departure times because their work is tied to East Coast business activity.

Estimation Results

To estimate the joint choice of mode and departure time, we used a multinomial logit model, one commonly used to estimate consumer choice among many alternatives, as is the case here.[23] Travelers' choices were assumed to be based on utility-maximizing behavior. Because this is a joint-

---

23. The multinomial logit joint-choice probabilities are given by

$$Prob_i = exp\,(\beta X_i) \,/ \sum_{j=1}^{J} exp\,(\beta X_j),$$

where $Prob_i$ is the probability of selecting mode–departure-time alternative i, parameters are denoted by β, explanatory variables are denoted by X_j, and J is the number of mode–departure-time alternatives including alternative i. We could not reject the multinomial logit specification, namely the independence of irrelevant alternatives (IIA) assumption, at high levels of confidence. Although we were estimating an "aggregate" logit model, the alternatives were not expressed as shares because this would disproportionately give larger weights to smaller cities and smaller weights to larger cities. Thus, each mode–departure-time alternative is simply a count, by distance block, of the number of commuters in a given urban area who chose that alternative.

choice model, the specification included influences on the choice of mode and departure time.[24]

Parameter estimates are presented in table 3-2 (the means for the modal attributes by commute distance block are in appendix B). Generally, the coefficients have their expected sign and are statistically precise. Higher fares on a given mode or at a given time discourage travelers from selecting that mode and time. As commuting distance increases, the effect of fares during the height of the peak travel period (7:30 a.m.–9:00 a.m.) is somewhat smaller than its effect during other time periods. This may be because long-distance commuters who travel during peak periods have less flexibility to alter their behavior in response to fare changes than people who commute long distances during other time periods.[25] We also found that the magnitude of the fare coefficient falls for the longest commutes, especially during the height of the peak travel period. This appears to be consistent with John Calfee and Clifford Winston's point that travelers often adjust to congestion through their decisions on where to reside. Thus travelers who live furthest from their workplaces tend to attach less disutility to travel cost and travel time than most travelers who live closer to work.[26]

Longer travel times for a given mode and departure time also discourage travelers from choosing that mode and time. The effect is stronger for all distances during the height of the peak travel period than during other times, which presumably reflects the greater utility that peak-period commuters attach to arriving promptly at their workplace. Travel time has the smallest effect on choice of mode and departure time for the shortest commutes,

---

24. A model that is potentially able to analyze a more structured set of behavioral responses than a joint-choice model is the nested logit model. This model also assumes travelers' choices of mode and departure time reflect utility-maximizing behavior. Applying the model to our problem first required us to estimate the determinants of mode choice and then to estimate the determinants of the choice of departure time, capturing the effect that the utility from modal alternatives has on choice of departure time through "log sums." The log sums are based on the coefficients of the mode-choice model. We found, however, that this model was inappropriate to use here because the log sums were statistically insignificant, which implied that *marginal* changes in the modal attributes of an urban transportation system do not affect departure-time choice probabilities. (Our findings were not altered when we reversed the sequencing of choices; that is, we first estimated a departure-time choice model and then estimated a mode-choice model, capturing the effect that the utility from departure-time alternatives has on mode-choice probabilities.)

25. This finding could also reflect differences in income.

26. John Calfee and Clifford Winston, "The Value of Automobile Travel Time: Implications for Congestion Policy," *Journal of Public Economics*, vol. 69 (July 1998), pp. 83–102.

regardless of when they occur. Commuters may be less sensitive to marginal changes in these travel times because they are so short or occur in uncongested conditions. We also found that the magnitude of the travel time coefficient drops sharply for the longest commutes, which again suggests that commuters adjust to congestion through their decisions on where to live.

Greater route coverage and service frequency increase the likelihood that a commuter will select a given mode and departure time. These effects are not sensitive to particular travel periods, but they do tend to become larger as commuting distances increase. This is plausible because commuters who live further from their workplaces may have a tendency to feel more isolated or stranded than commuters who live closer to work and thus place a greater value on accessibility and travel convenience (indeed, the effect of frequency for commuters who live the closest to their workplaces is statistically insignificant at conventional levels). In addition, differences in transit service across urbanized areas are more apparent or greater in the suburbs than in the city center. Finally, the negative sign of the carpool dummy indicates that, all else equal, commuters dislike driving to work with other people.[27]

The dummies for departure time show that travelers' preferences for departure times change in accordance with commute distance. Given their workplace and residential choices, commuters who travel less than ten miles to work prefer the 7:30 a.m.–8:00 a.m. departure time to the other periods, while commuters who travel more than ten miles want to leave for work earlier and prefer the 7:00 a.m.–7:30 a.m. departure time.[28] Workers in finance, real estate, and insurance prefer times between 8:00 a.m. and 10:00 a.m. because their business starts later in the day.[29] Workers in the continental United States appear to have some ties to East Coast business activity: the further west they live, the more they prefer earlier departure times, 5:00 a.m.–6:30 a.m., and the less they prefer later departure times, 8:00 a.m.–10:00 a.m. Workers in Alaska and Hawaii are apparently less

27. We caution that this dummy variable could be picking up the effect of omitted variables.

28. The dummies for departure time preference could also reflect the times that some commuters have to be at work.

29. We were unable to find any other occupations whose workers (such as farmers and miners) had distinct preferences for departure times. This may partly reflect our sample, which is composed of work trips in urbanized areas.

Table 3-2. *Joint Mode–Time Choice Parameter Estimates, by Distance Block*[a]

	Distance block				
Explanatory Variable	*Less than 1 mile*	*1–5 miles*	*6–10 miles*	*11–25 miles*	*More than 25 miles*
Fare per mile/annual household income (defined for 7:30–9:00 a.m., 0 otherwise)	-112.700 (3.260)	-200.800 (8.926)	-227.400 (11.540)	-223.900 (12.310)	-167.900 (8.897)
Fare per mile/annual household income (defined for other than 7:30–9:00 a.m., 0 otherwise)	-110.400 (3.191)	-201.000 (8.683)	-245.500 (11.700)	-263.800 (12.510)	-231.900 (9.629)
Total travel time per mile/annual household income (defined for 7:30–9:00 a.m., 0 otherwise)	-2.321 (255)	-13.290 (849)	-25.790 (1.513)	-29.950 (2.346)	-19.100 (3.295)
Total travel time per mile/annual household income (defined for other than 7:30–9:00 a.m., 0 otherwise)	-1.488 (218)	-9.688 (706)	-19.730 (1.204)	-23.880 (1.767)	-17.150 (2.468)
Route coverage (road or route miles per square mile of urbanized area)	0.105 (0.016)	0.178 (0.011)	0.165 (0.012)	0.250 (0.015)	0.336 (0.021)
Frequency of service (thousands of daily vehicle miles per road or route mile)	-0.039 (0.026)	0.102 (0.020)	0.270 (0.022)	0.311 (0.026)	0.308 (0.031)
Car pool mode dummy (1 if carpool alternative, 0 otherwise)	-1.718 (0.063)	-2.241 (0.055)	-2.521 (0.061)	-2.469 (0.063)	-2.184 (0.051)
Departure-time dummy (1 if 5:00–5:30 a.m., 0 otherwise)	-0.313 (0.140)	-0.143 (0.138)	0.019 (0.127)	0.234 (0.112)	0.281 (0.086)
Departure-time dummy (1 if 5:30–6:00 a.m., 0 otherwise)	0.298 (0.123)	0.528 (0.121)	0.572 (0.115)	0.646 (0.105)	0.523 (0.083)
Departure-time dummy (1 if 6:00–6:30 a.m., 0 otherwise)	0.983 (0.111)	1.321 (0.110)	1.595 (0.105)	1.807 (0.097)	1.329 (0.081)

Variable					
Departure-time dummy (1 if 6:30–7:00 a.m., 0 otherwise)	1.658 (0.100)	1.901 (0.101)	2.010 (0.098)	1.998 (0.093)	1.294 (0.079)
Departure-time dummy (1 if 7:00–7:30 a.m., 0 otherwise)	2.013 (0.098)	2.320 (0.100)	2.637 (0.098)	2.664 (0.096)	1.742 (0.088)
Departure-time dummy (1 if 7:30–8:00 a.m., 0 otherwise)	2.354 (0.103)	2.847 (0.152)	2.953 (0.179)	2.479 (0.217)	0.874 (0.242)
Departure-time dummy (1 if 8:00–8:30 a.m., 0 otherwise)	1.867 (0.162)	2.030 (0.203)	2.030 (0.233)	1.525 (0.275)	0.058 (0.301)
Departure-time dummy (1 if 8:30–9:00 a.m., 0 otherwise)	1.279 (0.165)	1.422 (0.205)	1.240 (0.236)	0.571 (0.279)	-1.085 (0.307)
Departure-time dummy (1 if 9:00–10:00 a.m., 0 otherwise)	1.260 (0.160)	0.993 (0.167)	0.717 (0.176)	0.326 (0.194)	-0.578 (0.203)
Percent employment in financial, insurance, or real estate (defined for 8:00–10:00 a.m., 0 otherwise)	6.180 (1.450)	6.724 (1.508)	5.708 (1.659)	5.298 (1.906)	7.020 (2.078)
Hours behind eastern standard time (defined for 5:00–6:30 a.m., 0 otherwise)	0.115 (0.036)	0.069 (0.034)	0.085 (0.032)	0.114 (0.029)	0.123 (0.025)
Hours behind eastern standard time (defined for 8:00–10:00 a.m., 0 otherwise)	-0.126 (0.042)	-0.207 (0.043)	-0.205 (0.044)	-0.171 (0.047)	-0.209 (0.041)
Alaskan or Hawaiian time (defined for 5:00–8:00 a.m., 0 otherwise)	-0.375 (0.127)	-0.497 (0.128)	-0.459 (0.131)	-0.486 (0.132)	-0.799 (0.106)
Log likelihood at zero	-22,480	-22,480	-22,480	-22,470	-22,460
Log likelihood at convergence	-16,430	-16,160	-15,930	-15,720	-16,630
Number of observations: 116 urbanized areas × 50 alternatives	5,800	5,800	5,800	5,800	5,800

Source: Authors' calculations.

a. Dependent variable is probability of selecting a given mode and departure time block. Standard errors in parentheses.

tied to East Coast business activity because they dislike departure times before 8:00 a.m.

Value of Travel Time

When most travelers choose their mode and departure time, they weigh their own cost and travel time but do not consider the costs those decisions impose on others through increased congestion. Efficient urban transportation policy calls for congestion tolls, based on the value of travelers' time, to force them to account for the congestion resulting from their choices. Therefore, the fare and travel time coefficients in our choice model are especially important to our analysis. A quantitative sense of their plausibility can be obtained by using them to calculate commuters' value of travel time.

Table 3-3 shows the value of time estimated in dollars per hour and, to facilitate comparisons with other studies, as a percentage of the average pretax hourly wage.[30] During the height of the peak travel period, 7:30 a.m.–9:00 a.m., the value of time as a share of wage ranges from 8 percent to 49 percent. In an extensive survey of estimates of the value of time, primarily based on *disaggregate* studies of mode choice, Kenneth Small found that the value of time ranges from 20 percent to 100 percent of the pretax wage and concluded that a reasonable average value is 50 percent.[31] Thus with the exception of the shortest commutes, which are much shorter than those used in the studies that Small surveys, our estimates are comparable with estimates in other studies. Medium-distance commuters value their time the most highly because the people facing the longest commutes have made residential location decisions (to be near suburban schools, for example) that attach less importance to longer travel times than many who prefer to live closer to work.[32] Another plausible finding is that the value of travel time diminishes during times outside the

30. The value of time estimates are obtained as the ratio of the travel time coefficient (in minutes) to the fare coefficient (in dollars), multiplied by sixty to yield an hourly value.

31. Small, *Urban Transportation Economics*, p. 44.

32. The unwillingness of commuters who do not travel very far to pay much to save time could reflect the fact that these commutes are very short or the possibility that they occur in uncongested conditions. Some people who value time very highly may have short commutes but not be in our sample because they walk to work.

Table 3-3. *Value of Travel Time for Peak and Off-Peak Travel, by Distance Block*

Distance block	Peak time (7:30–9:00 a.m.)		Off-peak time (times other than 7:30–9:00 a.m.)	
	Dollars per hour	Percent of average hourly earnings	Dollars per hour	Percent of average hourly earnings
Less than 1 mile	1.24	8	0.81	5
1–5 miles	3.97	24	2.89	18
6–10 miles	6.80	41	4.82	29
11–25 miles	8.03	49	5.43	33
More than 25 miles	6.83	41	4.44	27

Source: Authors' calculations.

height of the peak travel period.[33] Again, with the exception of the shortest commutes, estimates during these commute times are still within the range of previous estimates.[34]

Net Benefits of Urban Transportation Modes

We can also demonstrate the plausibility of our model by using it to estimate the net benefits that the public places on each mode of urban transportation under current pricing and service policies. These estimates indicate whether public subsidies to cover transit deficits can be economically justified.

We estimated the benefits that commuters derive from a mode by asking how much money they would have to be given (known as a compensating

33. MVA Consultancy and others, *The Value of Travel Time Savings* (Newbury, Berkshire, United Kingdom, 1987), and Calfee and Winston, "The Value of Automobile Travel Time," find that the value of time during congested travel conditions is higher than during uncongested conditions. Because it is likely that congestion will be greater during the height of the peak travel period than during other periods, these findings are consistent with our finding.

34. We can also calculate the marginal value of route coverage and frequency. For example, using the fare and route coverage coefficients, we found that a traveler's willingness to pay for an additional mile of route coverage provided by the urban transportation system was very small. This is plausible because the route coverage provided by the current system is extensive. A similar conclusion can be reached about the value of an additional trip provided throughout the day by the current urban system. Of course, the *difference* between the route coverage and frequency of autos and transit is an important influence on mode shares.

variation) when their preferred mode is eliminated to make them as well off as they were before the elimination.[35] We then subtracted the government subsidy to a mode from travelers' benefits to obtain net benefits. Subsidies for transit were calculated by subtracting the difference between revenues and total costs. Total costs were obtained for bus and rail by estimating cost functions.[36] In the case of the automobile's net benefits, we included the

35. The expression for the compensating variation (*CV*) is

$$CV = -\frac{1}{\beta_I}[\ln \sum_i exp\,(\beta X_i)\,]^{\beta X_i^f}_{\beta X_i^0},$$

where *i* denotes the mode–departure time alternatives, β denotes the set of coefficients from the mode–departure time choice model, *X* denotes the set of explanatory variables, the superscripts for *X* denote the value of the variables before mode–departure time alternatives are eliminated (*0*) and after they are eliminated (*f*). β_I is a conversion factor, equal to (minus) the fare coefficient divided by average household income, that is used to convert the results into monetary units per trip. See Kenneth A. Small and Harvey S. Rosen, "Applied Welfare Economics with Discrete Choice Models," *Econometrica*, vol. 49 (January 1981), pp 105–30. Because we estimated a fare coefficient for the height of the peak travel period and one for travel during other periods, we used an average value for the fare coefficient when constructing the conversion factor.

Because our estimation results are based on a sample of work trips, we made the following assumptions to obtain estimates that apply to trips for nonwork purposes as well. According to Alan E. Pisarski, *Nationwide Personal Transportation Survey: Travel Behavior Issues in the 90s* (Department of Transportation, Federal Highway Administration, 1992), p. 18, bus and rail work trips account for 40 percent of all bus and rail trips taken and automobile work trips account for 20 percent of all auto trips taken. (Of course, auto work trips account for an overwhelming percentage of all work trips taken.) Because the opportunity cost of being unable to make a nonwork trip is generally less than the opportunity cost of being unable to make a work trip, travelers are assumed to place less value on nonwork trips than on work trips. We thus assumed that nonwork trips are valued at 50 percent of the value of work trips. (We subject this assumption to sensitivity analysis later.) Using these figures, we obtained a *CV* per trip. Total trips are obtained by assuming work trips are 20 percent of all trips, as shown in Federal Highway Administration, *Survey of Travel Trends: 1990 NPTS* (Department of Transportation, 1992). Aggregate *CV* estimates were thus calculated by multiplying our estimated CV per trip by all trips.

36. Data for the bus and rail cost functions were from the Department of Transportation Section 15 database. We investigated whether it was appropriate to estimate a joint-cost function for transit systems that had bus and rail operations and a separate cost function for transit systems that just had bus operations. We found, however, that the interaction terms in the joint-cost function were statistically insignificant (the marginal cost of bus service was independent of rail's output and vice versa). We also found in a cost model for all bus systems that a dummy variable that indicated whether a bus system was in an urbanized area that also had a rail system was statistically insignificant. Indeed, the average load factors for bus systems in urbanized areas with and without rail systems were not statistically significantly different. Thus we estimated separate cost functions for bus and rail. Total costs include operating and capital costs. Capital costs were estimated by taking an average of capital expenditures from 1985 and 1990, multiplying this value by an assumed 10 percent interest rate, and adding depreciation. (Using a higher interest rate might be justified on the

reduction in government subsidies that would have gone to transit, but we are not able to account for any highway subsidies, given the way highway financial accounts are reported.[37] The calculations iteratively account for the effect of changes in service quality on travelers benefits that will result when a mode is eliminated (for example, when bus or rail is eliminated, auto congestion and travel times will increase, thus reducing traveler benefits). The changes in these travel times are calculated using the speed-flow curves described in appendix A. We assumed that the total number of trips is fixed. This assumption implies that we may be overstating the benefits of a mode because some people may prefer not to travel at all than to travel by their next-best alternative mode. Finally, we did not account for pollution and accident costs in the initial calculation, but we will account for these costs in subsequent calculations.

To be sure, the wholesale elimination of a mode such as automobiles would create changes in travel and living behavior far greater than could be captured in any model. Nonetheless, our findings give a qualitative sense of the net benefits that each mode provides to society. It is also important to bear in mind that in this exercise commuters' benefits from a mode are based on a comparison with the benefits they could derive from *alternative* transportation modes.

---

grounds that a number of systems are characterized by disinvestment, so that capital outlays understate true capital costs. Our findings, however, were not sensitive to plausible alternative interest rate assumptions.) The estimated cost function for bus systems is

Total cost = constant + 0.27 *passenger miles* + 0.05 *seat miles*, R^2 = .98.

Our central conclusions were not altered by using alternative functional forms or more elaborate specifications, that, for example, included factor prices and fixed effects.

Initial estimations indicated that heavy and light rail systems had somewhat different cost structures, but that these differences were not statistically significant. Thus, the estimated cost function for rail systems is

Total cost = constant + 0.17 *passenger miles* + 0.03 *seat miles*, R^2 = .98.

Again, our central conclusions were not altered by using alternative functional forms or more elaborate specifications.

37. Gabriel Roth, *Roads in a Market Economy* (Aldershot, England: Avebury Technical, 1996), points out that reported highway revenues and expenses of publicly owned roads do not include the depreciation of highway capital. Thus roads actually operate at a deficit, which suggests that our estimates of the net benefits of automobile travel are somewhat overstated because we do not include implicit highway subsidies.

Table 3-4. *Net Benefits of Urban Transportation Modes*

Billions of 1990 dollars unless otherwise specified

Mode	Consumer benefits per work trip (1990 dollars per trip)	Total consumer benefits	Government balances	Net benefits
Auto	4.97	161.9	21.7	183.6
Car pool	3.44	20.8	1.3	22.1
Bus	2.35	4.1	−9.9	−5.8
Rail	2.24	3.0	−3.0	0.0
Taxi	1.71	0.8	0.0	0.8

Source: Authors' calculations.

Table 3-4 shows, as expected, that travelers value automobile travel highly, since the annual net benefits from single-occupant autos and carpools exceed $200 billion. Eliminating bus service actually results in a net welfare gain to the public because the improvement in government balances (that is, the $9.9 billion deficit that is eliminated) exceeds the loss to consumers.[38] Under current policy, then, U.S. society as a whole would be better off on *aggregate* cost-benefit grounds if bus service ceased to be provided in its current form. (As we show later, this conclusion does not change if we account for pollution and safety costs.) This, of course, does not imply that public bus service in the United States cannot be justified on grounds of economic efficiency. That matter can be resolved only after we calculate the net benefits provided by bus systems when their prices and service are efficient. Our findings vary, of course, depending on urbanized area. Public bus transportation does generate net benefits in some cases.[39]

38. Our estimates of the benefits that travelers place on auto and bus travel can be compared with estimates obtained from a disaggregate mode choice model estimated by Debbie A. Niemeier, "Accessibility: An Evaluation Using Consumer Welfare," *Transportation*, vol. 24, no. 4 (1998), pp. 377–96, for King County, Washington. Niemeier estimates that King County commuters' value of the (single-occupant) automobile comes to $5.30 per work trip, which is very close to our estimate of $4.97 for commuters throughout major urban areas of the country. She also finds that commuters value bus travel at $0.87 per work trip, which is less than our estimate of $2.35, but this difference could arise because King County commuters' preferences for bus travel—and their system's fare and service offerings—are typically less than those of other urban commuters and systems.

39. John F. Kain and Zhi Liu, *Secrets of Success: How Houston and San Diego Transit Providers Achieved Large Increases in Transit Ridership* (Federal Transit Administration, Department

The value of rail service to commuters is offset by its subsidies, so its net social benefits are negligible. This raises the question of why new rail systems continue to be built and why existing ones are extended. The most likely answer, which we will return to later, is that political forces generate federal funds for urban rail systems, funds that are not determined in accordance with the benefits that accrue to people who use these systems. Rail systems could possibly generate moderate net benefits if their prices and service were efficient. Finally, taxicabs contribute nearly a billion dollars in net benefits to the public.

Summary

Because we seek to provide an overview of urban travel behavior throughout the country, we have departed from standard disaggregate mode choice modeling and developed an aggregate mode and departure-time choice model. Nonetheless, the estimates of parameters, calculations of the value of time, and estimates of each mode's net benefits indicate that the model does a credible job of capturing urban transportation preferences, which not surprisingly are strongly wedded to the automobile. Having formalized these preferences, we are now in position to estimate the social net benefits from an efficient urban transportation pricing and service policy.

---

of Transportation, May 1995), found that Houston and San Diego transit companies achieved large ridership increases during the 1980s by expanding service and reducing fares. But these improvements were made possible by extensive subsidies, so it is not clear whether the increases in ridership reflect an improvement in social welfare.

4

The Economic Effects of Net-Benefit Maximization

WE NOW ASK what an efficient urban transportation system in the public sector would look like and estimate the benefits that society would receive from this system. The prices and service levels called for under an efficient urban transportation policy, which we call net-benefit maximization, show that current urban transportation policy has produced serious economic inefficiencies. These are reflected in the large transit deficits financed by taxpayers and in significantly underpriced automobile travel. Net-benefit maximization would virtually eliminate the transit deficits and force auto travelers to pay for their contribution to congestion, but in exchange for much less frequent transit service and substantially higher prices for all modes of urban travel, including auto travel.[1] We will

---

1. Economists have made quantitative estimates of the effects of efficient urban transportation policies for specific modes in particular cities. For example, Steven A. Morrison, "A Survey of Road Pricing," *Transportation Research*, vol. 20A (March 1986), pp. 89–97, and Kenneth A. Small, *Urban Transportation Economics* (Philadelphia: Harwood Academic Publishers, 1992), summarize the welfare effects of optimal congestion tolls in various metropolitan areas. Marvin Kraus, "The Welfare Gains from Pricing Road Congestion Using Automatic Vehicle Identification and On-Vehicle Meters," *Journal of Urban Economics*, vol. 25 (May 1989), pp. 261–81, and John F. Kain, "The Impacts of Congestion Pricing on Transit and Carpool Demand and Supply," in National Research Council, *Curbing Gridlock: Peak-Period Fees to Relieve Traffic Congestion*, vol. 2: *Commissioned Papers* (Washington: National Academy Press, 1994), pp. 502–53, have analyzed the impact of congestion tolls on transit's market share. And Roberto Roson, "Revealed Preferences, Externalities and Optimal Pricing for Urban Transportation," Department of Economics, Ca' Foscari University, Venice, Italy, December 1996, and Paul Kerin, "Efficient Transit Management Strategies and Public Policies: Radial Commuter Arteries," Ph.D. dissertation, Harvard University, 1990, have estimated the economic effects of optimal pricing of urban transportation modes in Bologna, Italy, and Adelaide, Australia, respectively. Finally, Lyle C. Fitch and Associates, *Urban Transportation and Public Policy* (San Francisco: Chandler, 1964); John R. Meyer, John F. Kain, and Martin Wohl, *The Urban Transportation Problem* (Harvard University

postpone discussion of the political problems posed by the redistributive implications of a more efficient public urban transportation system until later chapters.

The Structure of the Analysis

Under efficient pricing, transit fares are equal to marginal cost. Optimal pricing of auto travel calls for marginal cost congestion tolls on highways, which can be assessed by automated vehicle identification systems without disrupting motorists' journeys or revealing their whereabouts. Each dimension of service is optimized when the marginal benefit from an additional unit of service is equal to its marginal cost. The dimensions of service that we found to affect travelers' behavior were travel time, frequency of service, and route coverage. In this analysis, we were able to optimize service frequency and optimize highway travel time by setting optimal congestion tolls. We also used sensitivity analysis to explore the potential benefits from optimizing vehicle capacity, but technical and conceptual problems prevented us from optimizing route coverage.[2]

Generally, the higher the quality of service, the more costly it is to provide. Thus one must link the marginal cost of transit with its service frequency to simultaneously optimize fares and service. Our approach was to estimate rail and bus cost functions that included a measure of frequency in the specification. The estimated (marginal) cost function provided optimal fares for a given frequency and enabled us to determine the combination of

---

Press, 1965); and Theodore E. Keeler, Kenneth A. Small, and associates, *The Full Costs of Urban Transport*, part 3: *Automobile Costs and Final Intermodal Cost Comparisons* (Institute of Urban and Regional Development, University of California, Berkeley, 1975), have compared the costs of urban transportation modes.

2. Our efforts to optimize route coverage were plagued by an absence of reliable construction cost data for rail systems and by the potential inaccuracies created by indivisibilities (that is, the optimal amount of route mileage could imply in some cases that only a fraction of a route is served). Randall J. Pozdena, *A Methodology for Selecting Urban Transportation Projects,* monograph 22 (University of California, Berkeley, 1975), has developed a residential collection model that could be used to optimize route coverage for an urban transportation analysis that uses disaggregate (origin-destination) travel data, but it is difficult to use this model here, given the level of aggregation of our data.

fare and frequency that maximizes net benefits.[3] Based on this cost model, the estimated marginal costs for bus service in our sample of urbanized areas range from $.43 to $1.09 per passenger mile (with an average of $.65), and the estimated marginal costs for rail service range from $.25 to $.51 per passenger mile (with an average of $.36).[4] As noted previously, rail has *relatively* lower marginal costs than bus systems because rail systems are already built and on average are located in corridors with greater traffic density. Some studies have found that in some urban areas it would have been far less costly to provide public transit service by bus instead of rail.[5]

Given bus and rail's extremely low load factors (in chapter 2 we determined that the average load factor of 14.3 percent for bus service and rail's average of 17.6 percent contributed to raising their operating costs per passenger mile above the cost of auto travel), it is not surprising that these marginal costs are so high. The fact that they significantly exceed transit fares (in table 3-1 average bus and rail fares are 13 cents and 17 cents, respec-

---

3. In chapter 3, note 36, the estimated cost function for bus operations is

$$Total\ cost = constant + 0.27\ passenger\ miles + 0.05\ seat\ miles,$$

where

$$seat\ miles = frequency \times average\ vehicle\ size \times route\ miles.$$

Thus,

$$Total\ cost = constant + 0.27\ passenger\ miles + 0.05\ (frequency \times average\ vehicle\ size \times route\ miles).$$

Average vehicle size and route miles are taken as exogenous data for each system, so we are able to determine the fare-frequency combination that maximizes net benefits.

Following the same procedure used for bus operations, the cost function for rail operations is

$$Total\ cost = constant + 0.17\ passenger\ miles + 0.03\ (frequency \times average\ vehicle\ size \times route\ miles).$$

4. *Average load factor = passenger miles/seat miles.* Thus using the estimated cost function for bus operations presented in note 3, we obtain

$$Total\ cost = constant + 0.27\ passenger\ miles + 0.05\ (passenger\ miles/average\ load\ factor).$$

We used this function to estimate the marginal cost of a passenger mile for bus service in each urbanized area in our sample. The same procedure was used to estimate the marginal cost of a passenger mile for rail service.

5. See, for example, José A. Gomez-Ibañez, "A Dark Side to Light Rail? The Experience of Three New Transit Systems," *Journal of the American Planning Association*, vol. 51 (Summer 1985), pp. 337–51; and John F. Kain, "Cost-Effective Alternatives to Atlanta's Costly Rail Rapid Transit System," *Journal of Transport Economics and Policy*, vol. 31 (January 1997), pp. 25–50.

tively, per passenger mile) is consistent with the large deficits currently incurred by these operations. Efficient pricing of transit at its current level of service and operating efficiency clearly calls for substantial increases in fares. If transit's service is optimized and its production efficiency is improved, the change in fares called for under efficient pricing is less clear.

Efficient automobile pricing requires optimal highway congestion tolls. We derived these tolls using speed-flow curves presented in appendix A. These tolls vary by time of day in accordance with traffic volume, the capacity of the road, and how much travelers value their time.[6] Their effect would be to increase automobile travelers' out-of-pocket cost to drive on congested roads, but those travelers who continued to use the road would benefit from higher travel speeds because there would be less congestion.

Efficient prices and service frequencies maximize net benefits, which are composed of travelers' welfare and transportation producers' "profits," including taxpayer subsidies.[7] Of course, most travelers are taxpayers, so they could still benefit as a group from an urban transportation system with, for example, higher transit fares, if transit subsidies were reduced and

---

6. As a practical and analytical matter, it is difficult to collect tolls for all routings of local roads, so we did not include the effects of optimal tolls on these roads. In addition, we did not assess optimal tolls on high-occupancy vehicles—buses, car pools, taxis—or heavy trucks. The implication of this decision is discussed later. Formally, the optimal toll, as derived by Theodore E. Keeler and Kenneth A. Small, "Optimal Peak-Load Pricing, Investment, and Service Levels on Urban Expressways," *Journal of Political Economy*, vol. 85 (February 1977), pp. 1–25, that corresponds to the speed-flow curve in appendix A is

$$Optimal\ toll = 0.13 \cdot Value\ of\ time \cdot$$
$$\frac{Vehicle\ miles}{Freeway\ miles} \cdot \frac{1}{\sqrt{471 - 0.26\ (vehicle\ miles/freeway\ lanes)}} \cdot$$
$$\frac{1}{(46 + \sqrt{471 - 0.26\ (vehicle\ miles/freeway\ lanes)})^2} \cdot$$

The value of time was calculated for peak and off-peak periods based on the estimates in our mode–departure time choice model.

7. More precisely, net benefits are given by

$$Net\ benefits = \Delta traveler\ benefits + \Delta congestion\ toll\ revenues + \Delta bus\ profits + \Delta rail\ profits.$$

The compensating variation (*CV*), which measures the change in travelers' benefits, is specified as in chapter 3, note 35, but the initial utility is utility under current prices and service, and the final utility is utility under optimal prices and service. *CV* captures the change in travelers' costs from congestion tolls.

returned to them through lower taxes or used for more socially desirable purposes. The only external cost we included in our base case is congestion. Data on accident and pollution costs are relatively crude, but we consider these in extensions to the model.[8]

Because the optimal prices and frequencies of each mode are interdependent, the net-benefit function is maximized by iterative optimization, as summarized in figure 4-1. For each distance block in a given urban area, each mode's prices and, where appropriate, service frequency are initially optimized one at a time.[9] For example, we first determined the congestion tolls that maximize net benefits, taking current transit prices and service as given. We then used our choice model for mode and departure time to account for travelers' mode and departure-time shifts in response to the change in auto prices. We then calculated the new levels of demand for each mode, the new travel times for the nonrail modes, and the new auto prices, and proceeded to determine the bus prices and frequency that maximize net benefits, taking the (optimal) congestion tolls and current rail prices and frequencies as given. We then accounted for mode and departure-time changes and recalculated the levels of demand for each mode, travel times for the nonrail modes, and congestion tolls and determined the rail prices and frequency that would maximize net benefits, taking the optimal auto and bus prices and optimal bus frequency as given. The process continued until an equilibrium was reached, at which point we calculated the change in consumer welfare, in bus, rail, and toll revenues, and in bus,

8. It has been claimed that employer-subsidized parking has contributed to congestion. We did not try to specify optimal workplace parking charges, given that we specified optimal congestion tolls. To the extent that parking charges are below marginal cost, this inefficiency should be treated as an employer-provided benefit that should be taxed.

9. It is not entirely clear whether it is appropriate to optimize travelers' waiting time when frequency is optimized. On the one hand, waiting time is constructed by assuming that it is one-half of the headway (time between vehicles) up to a maximum of fifteen minutes. Thus it might be reasonable to adjust waiting time when frequency changes. On the other hand, we recognize that the relation between waiting time and frequency that we used is not derived from optimizing behavior, but is a rule of thumb that appears to be consistent with current travel behavior and operations but might not be robust to dramatic changes in carrier service. Thus it might be reasonable to assume that travelers maintain their current waiting times. In any case, our findings did not change very much regardless of whether we adjusted waiting time when we optimized frequency, so in our base case we retained the current times.

Figure 4-1. *Equilibrium Pricing and Service Model*[a]

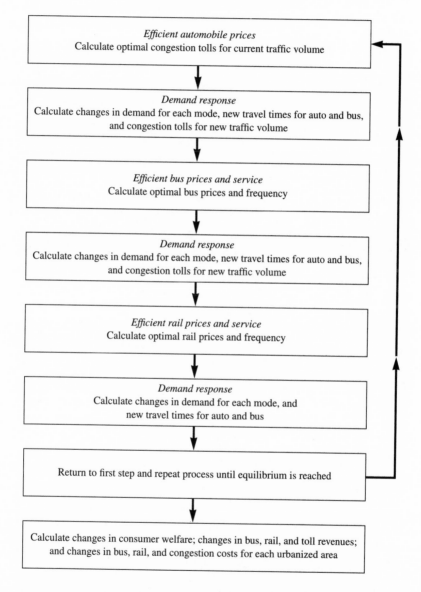

a. This algorithm applies to the case where we allowed bus travel times to change during peak and off-peak periods in proportion to changes in auto travel times. As noted in chapter 3 we did not include this modification in our final specification.

rail, and congestion costs for the urbanized area.[10] Estimates for the nation were obtained by summing these changes for the 116 urbanized areas in our sample.

To obtain estimates for all trips, we assumed, as before (see chapter 3, note 35), that travelers value nonwork trips at 50 percent of the value of work trips. We also assumed in our base case that bus and rail load factors are maintained at each system's average load factor, which effectively mandates a minimum frequency of service. This assumption can be interpreted as a political or physical constraint that we will relax in our sensitivity analysis.[11] We have pointed out that transit subsidies have been used to inflate wages and benefits and have influenced local governments to scrap transit equipment prematurely.[12] In addition, transit's extremely low load factors suggest that its capital and labor are being inefficiently used. Thus the estimated marginal costs of transit service based on current operating practices and technology are significantly higher than the marginal costs of fully efficient urban transit. Based on the work of John Pucher and others, our assumption was that transit marginal costs would be reduced by 15 percent in an efficient public urban transportation system.[13]

Finally, we point out that we were performing a short-run analysis because we did not attempt to characterize an optimal urban transportation network or optimal residential density in the long run. Thus, current highway capacity was taken as given, which is reasonable because the United States is unlikely to see massive investment in additional highway capacity, and disinvestment is not an option. Of course, this is not to say that current

10. The optimizations were performed using an IMSL subroutine. A thorough grid search indicated that the equilibrium that was attained generated the highest net benefits.

11. Herbert Mohring, "Optimization and Scale Economies in Urban Bus Transportation," *American Economic Review*, vol. 62 (September 1972), pp. 591–604, points out that expansions in frequency can reduce average waiting time and stimulate demand, which would increase load factors and lower fares. We did not analyze this effect in our base case because we held average load factors constant, but we will analyze this effect in our sensitivity analysis.

12. See Don H. Pickrell, "Rising Deficits and the Uses of Transit Subsidies in the United States," *Journal of Transport Economics and Policy*, vol. 19 (September 1985), pp. 281–98; Douglass B. Lee, *Evaluation of Federal Transit Operating Subsidies* (Department of Transportation, Transportation Systems Center, September 1987); and Brian A. Cromwell, "Federal Grant Policies and Public Sector Scrappage Decisions," Federal Reserve Bank of Cleveland, April 1990.

13. John Pucher, "Effects of Subsidies on Transit Costs," *Transportation Quarterly*, vol. 36 (October 1982), pp. 549–62. Also see José A. Gomez-Ibañez and John R. Meyer, *Going Private: The International Experience with Transport Privatization* (Brookings, 1993).

highway capacity is optimal. In addition, it is not likely that transit systems have optimized their route coverage, and our failure to do so here will cause us to understate the benefits from an efficient urban transportation system.

Findings

The effects on travelers, transportation providers, and taxpayers of setting prices and service frequency to maximize net benefits and of improving the cost efficiency of transit are presented in table 4-1. The annual net benefits from implementing only the pricing component of this policy total $6.6 billion (in 1990 dollars). This estimate was obtained by directly replacing each mode's current prices with its estimated marginal costs, accounting for differences in passenger miles and average load factors in each urbanized area, equilibrating based on current levels of service, and calculating the change in the net-benefit function.[14] Because optimal pricing calls for much higher prices, travelers lose about $13 billion, but these losses are more than offset by the reduced transit deficits and accumulated toll revenues that significantly improve the urban transportation budget balance.[15] Although one might argue that the average citizen is not likely to see greater net benefits in higher prices and lower deficits, studies have found that voters reward politicians for reducing government spending, so that travelers as a whole would derive benefits from an improved urban transportation budget balance.[16] In fact, these benefits would be even greater than we suggest because we did not include the cost of raising public funds to cover the deficit.

The prime source of the net benefits would be from automobile congestion tolls, and the benefits would be even greater if local roads, high-occupancy vehicles, and trucks were tolled and if we had been able to

14. The functions used to estimate bus and rail's marginal costs are given in note 4.

15. Congestion pricing provides benefits to peak-period auto travelers in the form of shorter travel time. The losses to consumers shown in table 4-1 include these benefits.

16. See Sam Peltzman, "Voters as Fiscal Conservatives," *Quarterly Journal of Economics*, vol. 107 (May 1992), pp. 327–61; and Clifford Winston and Robert W. Crandall, "Explaining Regulatory Policy," *Brookings Papers on Economic Activity: Microeconomics* (1994), pp. 1–49. Some may argue that these benefits could be affected by what the government does with the additional revenue.

Table 4-1. *Economic Effects of Net-Benefit Maximization and Marginal Cost Pricing Relative to Current Practice, by Mode*

Billions of 1990 dollars

Assumption and mode	Consumer benefits	Government balances	Net benefits
Marginal cost pricing only			
Auto, bus, and rail total	−13.3	19.9	6.6
Auto toll	−6.8	10.0	3.2
Bus	−3.6	5.8	2.2
Rail	−2.0	2.3	0.3
Net-benefit maximization (marginal cost pricing and optimal transit service frequency)			
Auto, bus, and rail total	−13.5	24.4	10.8
Bus	−3.6	9.7	6.1
Rail	−2.3	3.6	1.3
Net-benefit maximization with transit marginal costs reduced 15 percent			
Auto, bus, and rail total	−13.3	24.8	11.5

Source: Authors' calculations. The sum of the components of net benefits is not equal to the total change in net benefits because the compensating variation is nonlinear.

account for the long-run benefits from fewer distorted decisions on where homeowners and businesses choose to locate. Still another benefit from congestion pricing that we have not been able to account for is that by reducing stop-and-go traffic, efficient tolls could reduce the operating costs of all vehicles. Marginal cost pricing of bus service would bring in an additional $2.2 billion in annual net benefits.

An important conclusion to draw from these findings is that because efficiency will be improved if *any* mode's prices are aligned with its marginal costs, holding other modes' prices constant, one cannot reject marginal cost pricing by arguing that subsidies for a particular mode are justified because other modes are subsidized. The justification for subsidizing transit on efficiency grounds has been based to a large extent on this argument.[17]

Annual net benefits climb to $10.8 billion when prices and service frequency are set to maximize net benefits. The additional net benefits arise

17. There have also been attempts to justify transit subsidies on the grounds of transit's various economies, such as those of vehicle size and scale. But as pointed out, for example, by A. A. Walters, "Externalities in Urban Buses," *Journal of Urban Economics*, vol. 11 (January 1982), pp. 60–72, transit systems' failure to exhaust these economies probably reflects their inefficient operations.

because transit frequency is cut substantially, which lowers costs and further improves the budget balance. Indeed, bus and rail operations actually turn a small profit.[18] The additional loss in travelers' welfare from reduced service is partially offset by accompanying reductions in marginal cost fares.

Chapter 3 showed that public bus service does not appear to be economically justifiable for society as a whole under current pricing and service because aggregate benefits to travelers fall considerably short of subsidies from taxpayers. But a pricing and service policy based on net-benefit maximization would preserve public bus operations, albeit at a much smaller scale, and improve social welfare by $6.1 billion. This improvement exceeds the $5.8 billion that society would gain if bus service were simply eliminated. Rail's economic justification is also questionable under current policy, but rail can be justified economically—and increase aggregate social welfare by more than $1 billion—if its prices and service quality are set efficiently. Rail's modest net benefits, however, raise concerns about the social desirability of building new rail systems, even if these systems are operated efficiently. Finally, net benefits are even greater if transit can improve its cost efficiency. A modest 15 percent reduction in the marginal costs of bus and rail service could generate an additional $0.7 billion in benefits and increase the total benefits from an efficient urban transportation system to $11.5 billion (in 1990 dollars).

The extent to which urban transportation systems would change under optimal pricing and service frequency and improved operating efficiency is shown in table 4-2. Averaged over all systems, bus fares rise roughly fourfold, while frequency is cut more than two-thirds. Public bus transportation no longer runs a deficit, but this only appears to be possible with a national mode share of less than 1 percent, as compared with buses' current share of 5 percent. The changes in rail fares, frequencies, and mode share are qualitatively similar but less dramatic. Auto travel would also become more expensive, especially during peak travel periods in cities

18. The average profit for bus systems (or companies) is $177,000, while the average profit for rail systems is $14 million. Other researchers have also developed scenarios under which transit companies would be profitable; see, for example, Philip A. Viton, "On Competition and Product Differentiation in Urban Transportation: The San Francisco Bay Area," *Bell Journal of Economics*, vol. 12 (Autumn 1981), pp. 362–79.

Table 4-2. *Initial and Optimal Mode Shares, Auto Tolls, and Transit Attributes, by Mode*

Item	Initial value	Optimal value[a]
Mode share (percent)		
Auto	79.1	82.0
Car pool	14.3	15.6
Bus	4.7	0.9
Rail	1.1	0.6
Taxi	0.8	0.8
Auto tolls (cents per mile)		
12:00–5:00 a.m.	0	0
5:00–5:30 a.m.	0	0
5:30–6:00 a.m.	0	0
6:00–6:30 a.m.	0	1.8
6:30–7:00 a.m.	0	1.9
7:00–7:30 a.m.	0	4.8
7:30–8:00 a.m.	0	6.4
8:00–8:30 a.m.	0	2.6
8:30–9:00 a.m.	0	2.6
9:00–10:00 a.m.	0	0.8
Transit fares (cents per mile)		
Bus	13.2	55.2
Rail	17.4	34.8
Transit frequencies (number of times a route mile is covered per hour)		
Bus frequency	0.95	0.26
Rail frequency	20.80	12.40

Source: Authors' calculations.
a. Based on net benefit maximization with transit marginal costs reduced 15 percent.

with traffic congestion. But the share of autos and car pools still increase because travelers would find public transit's substantial fare increases and cutbacks in service more onerous than optimal congestion tolls. Thus net-benefit maximization would solve urban transportation's budgetary problems and significantly increase total welfare but would have only a modest impact on highway congestion.[19]

The effects of net-benefit maximization and improved transit operating efficiency on modal attributes and shares in selected cities are shown in

19. Although auto's mode share would increase, congestion and travel time would be reduced because some travelers would begin to use off-peak departure times or car pools. These changes, however, are not enough to produce large time savings (the largest decreases in average travel time are only a few minutes).

tables 4-3, 4-4, and 4-5. We have already noted that transit systems nation-wide differ greatly in age, size, and the state of their technology. Nevertheless, all systems exhibit the same inefficiencies. An efficient pol-icy would sharply raise all bus fares and, with the exception of the (pri-vately operated) Las Vegas system, substantially cut frequency of service everywhere.[20] Rail fares would also go up and, with the exception of the Atlanta, Pittsburgh, and Buffalo systems, service would be less frequent.[21] Optimal auto tolls for the most congested cities would be high—generally as much as 20 cents a mile during peak travel times (table 4-4).[22] Although the tolls would influence some people to travel at less congested times and to carpool, the increase in auto traffic caused by people who abandon tran-sit and return to their cars would mean only small reductions in travel time in all cities. The net result of the price and frequency changes under a pol-icy of net-benefit maximization would be to increase the shares of auto transportation and decrease the shares of transit operations (table 4-5).

Sensitivity Analysis

It is important to explore the sensitivity of our findings to various assumptions that we have made to this point. Because data on the choice of mode and departure time were available only for work trips, we were forced to make an assumption about the value that travelers placed on nonwork trips. Our assumption was that the trips were valued at 50 percent of the value assigned to work trips. Table 4-6 shows that the annual welfare gain from net-benefit maximization rises to nearly $15 billion if these trips are valued at 30 percent of the value of work trips. The welfare gain increases

20. Optimal frequency sometimes hits a lower-bound constraint of 0.21 trips per route mile per hour, or roughly 5 one-way trips per day.

21. Service improvements in Atlanta's MARTA system are constrained because the system's (matching) funds cannot come from state gasoline tax revenues: they must come from another source such as a local sales tax. Thus far only two of the five counties authorized to be served by MARTA have voted to impose the tax. See Edward Walsh, "Highway Bill Could Help, Hurt Atlanta," *Washington Post*, April 12, 1998, p. A4.

22. These tolls apply to an entire metropolitan area. Thus, for example, Atlanta has higher tolls than New York because its urbanized area is apparently more congested. According to our data, Atlanta's average automobile speeds are lower than New York's for given distances.

Table 4-3. *Initial and Optimal Transit Attributes, Selected Cities*

City	Bus fare (cents per mile)		Bus frequency (number of times a route mile is covered per hour)		Rail fare (cents per mile)		Rail frequency (number of times a route mile is covered per hour)	
	Initial	Optimal	Initial	Optimal	Initial	Optimal	Initial	Optimal
New York	27.4	52.9	1.96	0.23	16.8	37.3	69.4	10.1
Los Angeles	14.0	33.6	1.58	0.21	...	...	...	...
Chicago	21.9	46.6	1.83	0.21	9.4	30.5	33.8	29.9
San Francisco	10.3	48.7	1.33	0.21	11.8	34.5	30.8	6.4
Washington, D.C.	15.1	53.7	1.54	0.39	17.9	39.6	27.3	11.6
Dallas	12.7	51.6	1.04	0.21	...	...	...	...
Boston	16.6	61.9	1.63	0.34	15.2	37.4	22.4	10.5
Atlanta	11.7	60.0	1.58	0.22	7.1	38.0	26.6	30.9
Pittsburgh	12.8	40.6	1.21	0.21	9.6	30.7	4.0	6.6
New Orleans	13.4	33.8	2.00	0.21	15.8	28.2	4.6	1.3
Buffalo	20.0	39.6	0.63	0.21	18.2	34.3	9.3	13.2
Las Vegas	26.0	51.5	0.83	0.87	...	...	...	...
Toledo	7.8	58.2	0.92	0.21	...	...	...	...
Charlotte	10.5	48.9	1.13	0.62	...	...	...	...
Peoria	10.0	62.7	0.54	0.21	...	...	...	...
Anchorage	8.8	74.4	0.63	0.31	...	...	...	...
Montgomery	18.9	65.9	0.67	0.21	...	...	...	...

Source: Authors' calculations.

Table 4-4. *Optimal Auto Tolls, Selected Cities, by Daily Morning Time Period*

Cents per mile

City	12:00–5:00	5:00–5:30	5:30–6:00	6:00–6:30	6:30–7:00	7:00–7:30	7:30–8:00	8:00–8:30	8:30–9:00	9:00–10:00
New York	0	0	0	3	3	11	16	5	4	1
Los Angeles	1	1	1	12	12	18	24	16	16	14
Chicago	0	0	0	3	3	16	45	4	3	1
San Francisco	0	0	0	12	12	11	16	16	16	2
Washington, D.C.	0	0	0	3	3	12	17	4	4	1
Dallas	0	0	0	3	3	15	25	4	3	1
Boston	0	0	0	2	2	26	30	4	3	1
Atlanta	0	0	0	3	3	14	22	4	4	1
Seattle	0	0	0	4	4	12	20	5	5	1
Pittsburgh	0	0	0	1	1	1	2	1	1	0
New Orleans	0	0	0	1	1	4	5	2	2	1
Buffalo	0	0	0	1	1	1	1	1	1	0
Las Vegas	0	0	0	2	2	19	25	3	3	1
Toledo	0	0	0	1	1	1	2	1	1	0
Charlotte	0	0	0	3	3	11	13	4	4	1
Peoria	0	0	0	0	0	0	1	0	0	0
Anchorage	0	0	0	1	1	1	2	1	1	0
Montgomery	0	0	0	1	1	1	2	1	1	0

Source: Authors' calculations.

Table 4-5. *Initial and Optimal Mode Shares, Selected Cities*

City	Auto		Car pool		Bus		Rail		Taxi	
	Initial	Optimal	Initial	Optimal	Initial	Optimal	Initial	Optimal	Initial	Optimal
New York	75.1	78.8	12.4	13.7	2.9	1.8	7.8	3.9	1.8	1.8
Los Angeles	74.9	69.9	20.5	25.8	2.1	1.8	...	...	2.6	2.5
Chicago	71.7	76.6	12.9	15.1	2.8	1.2	11.0	5.5	1.7	1.6
San Francisco	75.1	77.2	13.5	15.8	5.1	2.1	5.8	4.4	0.6	0.6
Washington, D.C.	74.8	80.6	11.4	13.0	5.6	1.8	7.8	4.2	0.5	0.5
Dallas	80.5	79.8	15.3	18.1	2.9	0.7	...	...	1.3	1.5
Boston	72.4	78.0	11.8	14.3	4.4	1.3	10.5	5.4	0.9	1.0
Atlanta	69.2	78.8	12.1	15.4	3.7	0.6	14.5	4.7	0.5	0.6
Seattle	76.6	78.2	13.6	16.7	7.0	1.9	2.5	2.9	0.3	0.3
Pittsburgh	76.1	80.1	13.5	14.4	4.4	1.6	4.7	2.7	1.3	1.2
New Orleans	78.7	80.2	16.6	17.1	3.6	1.6	0.8	0.7	0.4	0.4
Buffalo	79.2	82.2	13.2	13.7	3.0	1.4	4.1	2.2	0.6	0.5
Las Vegas	78.2	81.2	15.3	17.2	6.3	1.4	...	...	0.2	0.2
Toledo	79.4	83.5	13.2	14.1	6.1	0.9	...	...	1.4	1.4
Charlotte	80.0	82.6	13.5	15.5	5.9	1.2	...	...	0.6	0.7
Peoria	80.7	84.8	13.1	13.8	5.6	0.7	...	...	0.6	0.6
Anchorage	75.3	84.6	11.6	13.2	12.7	1.6	...	...	0.5	0.5
Montgomery	81.4	84.4	14.2	15.0	4.3	0.4	...	...	0.2	0.2

Source: Authors' calculations.

Table 4-6. *Changes in Consumer Benefits, Government Balances, and Net Social Benefits under Assumptions about the Value of Nonwork Trips and Load Factors*[a]

Billions of 1990 dollars

Assumption	Consumer benefits	Government balances	Net benefits
Net-benefit maximization, base case (nonwork trips valued at 50 percent of work trips)	−13.3	24.8	11.5
Nonwork trips valued at 30 percent of work trips	−9.8	24.7	14.9
Nonwork trips valued at 70 percent of work trips	−16.5	24.6	8.1
Load factors allowed to rise to 50 percent of capacity	−12.6	24.8	12.2

Source: Authors' calculations.

a. Marginal cost pricing and optimal transit service frequency with transit marginal costs reduced 15 percent. Negative sign indicates loss of of benefits.

under this assumption because travelers' losses from higher fares and less frequent service are reduced, while the improvements in the transportation budget are essentially unchanged. If nonwork trips are valued at 70 percent of the value of work trips, travelers' annual net benefits fall to $8 billion, which is still a sizable gain in social welfare.

In our base case we assumed that bus and rail load factors would be equal to each system's average load factor. This assumption obviously understates the benefits from net-benefit maximization because it is likely that an efficient urban transit system would make much greater use of its capacity than the current system. We considered how net benefits would change if bus and rail operations were able to increase their load factors to as much as 50 percent. Note that in this simulation travelers' waiting times are affected when we optimize frequency (for example greater frequencies reduce waiting time). In addition, fares are adjusted in accordance with changes in load factors and frequencies (for example, fares fall as load factors increase and rise as frequencies increase). Under these conditions, travelers would gain $0.7 billion from lower fares and annual net benefits rise to $12.2 billion. Although we found that service would be somewhat less frequent, the higher load factors would enable transit systems to maintain their budget balance with lower fares.[23] Bus and rail operations' more efficient use of capacity would also enable them to regain some market share (bus operations' share would expand from 0.9 percent to 2 percent and rail's from 0.6 percent to 0.8 percent). Transit's potential to improve its efficiency suggests that it could become a much more important factor in urban transportation than appears possible given its current level of efficiency.

Accidents and Pollution

An efficient urban transportation policy should also take account of the social costs of accidents and pollution. Although these costs are difficult to measure precisely, our estimates suggest that they would not have much effect on our findings. First, it is not clear that it is appropriate to charge travelers for vehicle accidents because travelers absorb most of these costs through various types of insurance.[24] Perhaps the only cost that travelers involved in accidents do not bear are the delays they cause other travelers. This cost would be difficult to assess, and charging for it would have little effect on travelers' behavior. Nonetheless, we constructed the total costs of accidents and fatalities for each mode and found that marginal accident costs are 15.5 cents per (auto) vehicle mile, 12.4 cents per bus passenger mile, and 8.5 cents per rail passenger mile.[25] Under net-benefit maximization, total accident costs actually fall $0.7 billion—from $78.8 billion to

23. Mohring, "Optimization and Scale Economies in Urban Bus Transportation," pointed out that increases in frequency can reduce average waiting time and stimulate demand, which would increase load factors and lower costs. Although we allowed for this possibility, optimization in our context called for reductions in transit frequency.

24. A motorist who is allegedly responsible for an accident involving pedestrians or other vehicles is also vulnerable to civil suits.

25. Automobile fatalities are from the *Vital Statistics of the United States 1990*, vol. 2: *Mortality Part B* (Department of Health and Human Services, 1994), and automobile injuries are derived from the *Costs of Highway Crashes* (Federal Highway Administration, 1991). Transit fatalities and injuries are from the Department of Transportation Section 15 database. Total accident costs for each mode were then derived using the *Costs of Highway Crashes*. We ran simple regressions of total accident costs on vehicle miles for automobiles and passenger miles for bus and rail operations. The coefficients enabled us to calculate the marginal accident costs of an additional auto, bus, or rail passenger mile and thus the total accident costs for each mode in each urbanized area.

Table 4-7. *Changes in Consumer Benefits, Government Balances and Net Social Benefits under Three Assumptions about Accidents and Pollution*[a]

Billions of 1990 dollars

Assumption	Consumer benefits	Government balances	Accident or pollution costs	Net benefits
Net benefit maximization (base case with transit marginal costs reduced 15 percent)	−13.30	24.80	. . .	11.50
Accident costs included in optimization	−13.16	24.62	0.74	12.20
Pollution costs included in optimization, but not charged to travelers	−13.18	24.71	−0.42	11.10
Pollution costs included in optimization, and charged to travelers	−27.99	24.99	14.55	11.55

Source: Authors' calculations.

a. Marginal cost pricing and optimal transit service frequency with transit marginal costs reduced 15 percent. Negative sign indicates loss of of benefits.

$78.1 billion—because the increase in auto accident costs would be offset by a decrease in bus and rail accident costs (table 4-7).

It is possible to construct a plausible (upper-bound) pollution charge to travelers. Kenneth Small and Camilla Kazimi have estimated that the pollution costs from automobiles average 3 cents per mile. We assumed the pollution costs from buses average 6 cents per mile.[26] The results presented in table 4-7 show that charging travelers for these costs has a very small effect on the welfare gains from net-benefit maximization. Under the first assumption about pollution, costs are included in the tabulation of net benefits (thus slightly impeding welfare gains from the base case), but travelers are not explicitly charged for these costs. Including pollution costs in the marginal cost charges to auto and bus travelers, as is done under the second

26. Kenneth A. Small and Camilla Kazimi, "On the Costs of Air Pollution from Motor Vehicles," *Journal of Transport Economics and Policy*, vol. 29 (January 1995), pp. 7–32. The figure for automobiles applies to the Los Angeles area and thus is higher than estimates for other urbanized areas. No precise cost estimate is available for bus pollution, but it is acknowledged that the cost is at least twice as high as the cost of auto emissions. Rail transit also has some pollution costs from electricity generation, but we are not aware of estimates of these costs and thus did not include them here.

pollution assumption, leads to little change in net welfare because the gains to the public from greater revenues and less pollution are virtually offset by losses to travelers from higher fares.[27]

Qualifications

Notwithstanding our sensitivity analyses and extensions, the limitations of our model and our use of aggregate data cause us to overstate the losses to travelers in some respects and generally understate the net benefits from an efficient public urban transportation policy. Travelers' losses are over-stated because our model does not allow them to adjust the number of trips they take in response to optimized prices and levels of service. For example, faced with much higher bus fares and less frequent service, some travelers might prefer to take fewer trips rather than switch to auto travel or alter departure times. In addition, we were unable to consider the benefits that travelers might receive if, in the long run, they (efficiently) altered their destinations or even changed residential or workplace locations in response to changes in an urban transportation system's prices and service quality.

The use of aggregate data prevents us from identifying the benefits that travelers and carriers would receive if carriers were able to achieve the most efficient route coverage. Of course, some travelers would probably find that their routes were abandoned, but these losses could be temporary if new carriers were allowed to enter the market. Transit's economic viability may also be greater than our analysis suggests because aggregate data mask its greater efficiencies in high-density metropolitan traffic corridors. Finally, our analysis does not fully account for the fact that congestion costs rise more than proportionately with traffic. Because we averaged the effects of

27. Because of its low load factor, transit consumes far more energy than automobiles per passenger trip. Therefore the auto mode share would expand under a pricing policy designed to promote energy conservation; see Robert Cervero, "Perceptions of Who Benefits from Public Transportation," *Transportation Research Record*, vol. 936 (1983), pp. 15–19; and Gordon Fielding, "Transit in American Cities," in Susan Hanson, ed., *The Geography of Urban Transport*, 2d ed. (Guildford Press, 1995), pp. 287–304. Auto and bus noise costs per passenger mile are less than 1 cent, so accounting for these costs would have little effect on our findings. See Todd Litman, "Transportation Cost Analysis: Techniques, Estimates, and Implications," Victoria Transport Policy Institute, Victoria, British Columbia, January 1995, p. 3.11-3.

congestion pricing over thousands of origin-destination pairs in an urbanized area, we have understated the benefits from congestion tolls on highly congested arterials and highways.

Summary

James Q. Wilson has pointed out that public urban transportation policy has been bedeviled by attempting to subsidize travel choices while at the same time reducing the costs attached to them.[28] The result has been an urban transportation system riddled with large public deficits and unabated congestion. This chapter has outlined a vision of what public urban transportation systems in the United States would look like if prices and service frequency were set efficiently and if public transit improved its operating efficiency. This policy, known as net-benefit maximization, would benefit the public by eliminating transit deficits, but it would call for higher urban transportation prices and less frequent service. And it shows that efficient urban transportation would require *more*, not less, automobile travel (spread more evenly throughout the day), a result contrary to the vision of urban transportation policy since the 1960s.

Notwithstanding the economic benefits from net-benefit maximization, it is hard to imagine policymakers lining up to support a policy that will *raise* the price of urban transportation. Political reality must be faced. But economic reality must be faced too—the empirical evidence strongly suggests that the public is paying a high price for a seriously flawed urban transportation policy. Uncovering the source of these flaws is our next step to envisioning an alternative that can improve the efficiency of our urban transportation system while meeting distributional concerns that low-income travelers will not be harmed in the process.

28. James Q. Wilson, "Cars and Their Enemies," *Commentary*, July 1997, pp. 17–23.

5

Sources of Inefficiencies

POLICYMAKERS do not just happen to create inefficiencies. When economists estimate large welfare losses stemming from public policies as if the losses were simple oversights that officials could correct by paying closer attention to what they are doing, it is the economists, not the officials, who are not paying attention. This chapter attempts to chip away at this type of ignorance by developing a model to identify the political forces most responsible for the inefficiencies in urban transit pricing and service that were documented in chapter 4. It also identifies the factors that contribute to the inefficiencies in automobile travel. We will then be in a position to assess whether urban transportation policymakers would actually take significant steps to make public systems more efficient and less reliant on taxpayer subsidies.

Sources of Inefficiencies in Transit

One generally expects politics to have a major influence on public policy. And theories abound as to why this influence will create economic inefficiencies.[1] Without drawing explicitly on a particular theory, we can identify at least three ways in which politics is likely to cause urban transit prices and service to deviate from optimality. First, although we noted in

1. Roger Noll, "Economic Perspectives on the Politics of Regulation," in Richard Schmalensee and Robert D. Willig, eds., *Handbook of Industrial Organization,* vol. 2 (Amsterdam: North-Holland, 1989), pp. 1253–87, discusses various political theories of regulation that illustrate the connection between political influences and economic inefficiencies.

chapter 1 that government subsidies largely accrue to transit managers and suppliers of transit labor and capital, some of the funds undoubtedly go to keep fares below marginal costs and to expand service beyond what can be supported without subsidies. Second, as we discussed in chapter 2, various policymaking entities determine transit prices and service and receive federal funds. Some may be less capable than others of carrying out efficient policies or more willing to sacrifice efficiency in pursuit of other goals.[2] Finally, such varied transportation constituencies as high-income commuters, business developers, and the elderly could influence policymakers to benefit them at the expense of other members of society by lowering prices and expanding service to inefficient levels.[3]

We have estimated simultaneous equations models of transit prices, service frequency, and route coverage to determine the effect of subsidies, policymaking entities, and constituents on them, and have used the models to determine how much of the social welfare loss from transit pricing and service inefficiencies can be explained by these political influences. Because of the limited guidance that economic theory brings to help our specifications and the absence of comparable empirical work, we recognize that our models offer only preliminary empirical evidence on the political and economic determinants of transit attributes.[4] Our basic findings, however, appear to be consistent with informal observations and anecdotal

2. David W. Jones Jr., *Urban Transit Policy: An Economic and Political History* (Prentice-Hall, 1985), points out that discretionary transit funds tend to go to the entities that are having the most severe problems with ridership or experiencing the greatest financial difficulty. Policymakers' goals could include promoting transit as part of some general ideology or rewarding some interest group in return for political support.

3. John F. Kain, "Choosing the Wrong Technology: Or How to Spend Billions and Reduce Transit Use," *Journal of Advanced Transportation*, vol. 21 (Winter 1988), pp. 197–213, and Peter Gordon and Harry Richardson, "Notes from Underground: The Failure of Urban Mass Transit," *Public Interest*, vol. 94 (Winter 1989), pp. 77–86, point out that cities and municipal transit agencies seek state and federal funding, states seek federal funding, and local interests lobby all policymakers. For example, meetings of the Los Angeles Metropolitan Transportation Authority attract more lobbyists than do all the offices of the state legislature in Sacramento.

4. Gary R. Nelson, "An Econometric Model of Urban Bus Transit Operations," in Institute for Defense Analysis, *Economic Characteristics of the Urban Public Transportation Industry* (Department of Transportation, 1972), chap. 4, investigates alternative hypotheses about bus company objectives, including ridership maximization, bus miles maximization, and so on but does not attempt to analyze the political forces that might influence these objectives.

evidence on the extent of inefficiency that is caused by political influences on urban transit policy.

Specification and Estimation of Bus Transit Attributes

Our framework posits that bus prices, route coverage, and frequency of service in an urban area are determined by the economic characteristics of the system, its operating environment, and the political influences on it that are reflected in the policymaking entity, the extent of government subsidies, and the characteristics of transportation constituents.

Fare or price equations, and the economic variables that should be used as cost and demand controls in them, have had a long tradition in transportation economics.[5] The variables we used to control for cost influences on fares are average trip distance, route density, vehicle capacity, and operating expenses. We also included population density to control for potential demand. Increasing these variables should raise fares. The exception is increases in route density, which, by lowering costs, should lower fares. In addition to these standard variables, we controlled for the amount of bus service in an urbanized area provided by private and purchased (contracted) bus transportation to see whether alternative suppliers have distinct effects on fares. Finally, we included each urbanized area's government subsidy, which, if increased, should lower fares, as indicated earlier.

Our bus fare equation extends previous transportation fare equations by controlling for the policymaking entity that is responsible for fare decisions in an urbanized area. As chapter 2 explained, identifying the actual decisionmaker is not straightforward because a number of entities could indirectly influence decisions—for example, a transit authority may have responsibility for setting fares, but the governor may indirectly influence its decisions because he or she appoints the members of the transit authority.

5. The specification of pricing models evolved from transportation cost models of the type pioneered by John R. Meyer, "Some Methodological Aspects of Statistical Costing as Illustrated by the Determination of Rail Passenger Costs," *American Economic Review*, vol. 48 (May 1958), pp. 209–34.

Our specification therefore included the policymaking entity with explicit authority to set fares—a state (usually the governor's office), city (usually the mayor's office), county, metropolitan planning organization, or transit authority—and policymaking entities that could influence fares either because they appoint members of the decisionmaking entity or because they are recipients of federal mass transportation funds.[6]

We also controlled for the socioeconomic composition—income, age, and ethnicity—of a bus systems' users (that is, transportation constituents as a percentage of the eligible voting age population).[7] We categorized the population as lower income (annual household income less than $20,000), middle income ($20,000 to $75,000), and upper income (greater than $75,000). We also decomposed middle income into lower-middle income ($20,000 to $50,000) and upper-middle income ($50,000 to $75,000). Travelers younger than age twenty-five were classified as young; those older than sixty-five were classified as elderly. Finally, the ethnic groups we considered were blacks and Hispanics and Asian Americans.[8] If one applies

6. It could also be argued that the effects of policymaking entities vary in accordance with such matters as length of time in office, political party, the size and composition of technical and administrative staffs, and so on. We incorporated these characteristics (and others) of a decisionmaking entity by interacting them with the dummy variable that identified the decisionmaker, but we found that they were statistically insignificant. Finally, the effects of policymaking entities might also vary with the characteristics of urban areas. For example, a transit authority empowered to set fares may have a greater influence on fares in a metropolitan area dominated by a large central city than in one composed of several small cities. However, we were unable to detect that the effects of policymaking entities were sensitive to the characteristics of an urban area.

7. Seventeen-year-olds are also included in this population. We also specified classifications of travelers by education levels, industry occupation, whether they had a disability, and so on, but these classifications were not statistically significant. One might interpret bus users' characteristics as proxies for demand elasticities (or values of travel time) and thus argue that these variables should be classified as conventional economic variables. This could be reasonable if bus prices and service were determined in unregulated markets, in which case profit-maximizing bus companies could be expected to take account of consumers' socioeconomic characteristics. It is highly unlikely, however, that this is the reason policymakers' decisions might be influenced by users' characteristics. In fact, specifications of bus user groups as a percentage of eligible voters outperformed specifications of bus user groups as a percentage of all bus users in terms of statistical significance and goodness of fit, which suggests that the influence of bus user groups is more accurately captured when they are characterized as potential voters rather than just bus users per se. Finally, this analysis is motivated by evidence developed in chapter 4 that urban transit *is* characterized by serious pricing and service inefficiencies. Transit's constituents are obviously a potential cause of these inefficiencies.

the terminology of the Chicago model of regulation, the policymaking entities can be thought of as suppliers of regulation, in this case regulated bus fares, and the bus users can be thought of as demanders of regulation.[9]

It is reasonable to expect that bus route coverage and service frequency would be influenced by at least some of the same economic variables that influence fares. Coverage and frequency are also likely to be affected by transit policymaking entities and the socioeconomic composition of bus users. Of course, it is difficult to indicate a priori how these influences might vary, if at all, by bus attribute.

Preliminary estimation revealed that certain variables had a statistically significant effect on some attributes but not on others. We generally incorporated these findings (that is, eliminated the highly insignificant variables from the appropriate equations); specified bus fares, route coverage, and frequency as a system of equations; and obtained parameter estimates by three-stage least squares estimates (table 5-1).[10]

Generally, the parameter estimates indicate, as expected, that the determinants of bus fares, route coverage, and service frequency go beyond conventional economic influences to include government subsidies, the policymaking entities, and transportation constituents' characteristics. Subsidies,

8. Blacks and Hispanics are combined as one group on the basis of similar statistical findings in our analysis. There are other interest groups, for example, construction companies, besides travelers that might receive benefits from transit policymakers, but we did not find that these groups directly had a statistically significant effect on fares, frequency of service, or route coverage. Of course, a specific policymaker's effect on fares or service may capture benefits that are partly targeted to other groups in addition to travelers (for example, a state might promote lower fares to increase transit ridership and transit employment.) Government subsidies could also have this type of effect.

9. It is important to clarify the difference between the effect of policymaking entities on bus attributes and the effect of transportation constituents. The coefficients of the policymaking entities capture their competence and general goals (for instance, to promote a larger bus system). They do not capture how their competence or goals affect the welfare of particular socioeconomic groups. Indeed, we were not able to identify statistically any interaction effects between specific policymaking entities and constituent groups. The coefficients for the constituent groups capture either a particular group's general influence on policymakers or how that group may be affected by policymakers' broad social goals, such as increasing urban mobility.

10. In a few instances we report a statistically imprecise coefficient for a variable if that finding per se is of particular interest. Three-stage least squares produces consistent and efficient parameter estimates that account for the correlation of the attribute equations' error terms and for the fact that some of the variables in the attribute equations are endogenous (namely, route coverage, a dependent variable for one equation, is also used as an independent variable in the fare and frequency equations).

Table 5-1. *Three-Stage Least Squares Estimates of Bus Attribute Equations*[a]

Variable	Coefficient
Bus fare equation	
Constant	−0.4799
	(0.2938)
Average bus work trip distance (miles)	0.0568
	(0.0122)
Average number of seats per vehicle (seats)	0.0128
	(0.0045)
Operating expense per passenger mile (dollars per mile)	0.0124
	(0.0047)
Population density in UZA (population per square mile)	0.8507E-04
	(0.2947E-04)
Route coverage (directional bus route miles per square mile in UZA)	−0.0779
	(0.0213)
Total revenue miles from purchased transportation (percent)	−0.2861
	(0.1536)
Total revenue miles from private transportation entity (percent)	−0.0486
	(0.0652)
Subsidy (Nonpassenger fare revenue per maximum-service vehicle, thousands of dollars per vehicle)	−0.0004
	(0.0002)
Local entity makes fare decisions (1 if local entity makes decisions, 0 otherwise)	−0.1266
	(0.0357)
Governor-appointed transit authority makes fare decisions (1 if governor-appointed transit authority makes decisions, 0 otherwise)	−0.1122
	(0.0499)
Bus commuters under age 25 as percent of persons older than 16	−25.685
	(13.576)
Asian-American bus commuters as percent of persons older than 16	−12.958
	(2.232)
Middle-income bus commuters as percent of persons older than 16	15.430
	(5.343)
Bus route coverage equation	
Constant	0.4772
	(0.3213)
Population density in UZA (population per square mile)	0.0009
	(0.0001)
Total revenue miles from purchased transportation (percent)	−1.0097
	(0.3055)
Total revenue miles from private transportation entity (percent)	−0.7026
	(0.3708)

Table 5-1. *Three-Stage Least Squares Estimates of Bus Attribute Equations*[a]
(Continued)

Variable	Coefficient
Bus route coverage equation (continued)	
Local entity makes route decisions (1 if local entity makes decisions, 0 otherwise)	–0.3832 (0.2441)
Local entity receives federal mass transit grant money (1 if local entity receives grant money, 0 otherwise)	–0.4080 (0.1531)
Governor makes route decisions (1 if governor makes decisions, 0 otherwise)	0.9961 (0.6089)
Lower-income bus commuters as percent of persons older than 16	244.224 (44.032)
Upper middle-income bus commuters as percent of persons older than 16	101.934 (44.748)
Black and Hispanic bus commuters as percent of persons older than 16	–144.559 (21.117)
Bus frequency equation	
Constant	1.402 (1.003)
Population density in UZA (population per square mile)	0.0015 (0.0004)
Operating expense per passenger mile (dollars per passenger mile)	–0.1414 (0.0635)
Route coverage (directional bus route miles per square mile in UZA)	–0.9855 (0.2809)
Total revenue miles from purchased transportation (percent)	2.358 (0.6028)
Total revenue miles from private transportation entity (percent)	1.194 (0.8307)
Subsidy (nonpassenger fare revenue per maximum service vehicle, thousands of dollars per vehicle)	0.0094 (0.0024)
Governor makes route decisions (1 if governor makes decisions, 0 otherwise)	1.302 (1.033)
Governor-appointed transit authority makes route decisions (1 if governor-appointed transit authority makes decisions, 0 otherwise)	2.764 (0.963)
Popularly appointed transit authority makes route decisions (1 if popularly appointed transit authority makes decisions, 0 otherwise)	2.776 (1.061)

Table 5-1. *Three-Stage Least Squares Estimates of Bus Attribute Equations*[a]

Variable	Coefficient
Bus frequency equation (continued)	
Local entity makes route decisions (1 if local entity makes decisions, 0 otherwise)	1.195
	(0.8728)
Lower-income bus commuters as percent of persons older than 16	365.436
	(123.647)
Lower middle-income bus commuters as percent of persons older than 16	383.519
	(207.120)
Upper middle-income bus commuters as percent of persons older than 16	−702.811
	(453.693)
Asian-American bus commuters as percent of persons older than 16	206.448
	(51.575)
R^2 bus fare equation	0.66
R^2 bus route coverage equation	0.63
R^2 bus frequency equation	0.79

Source: Authors' calculations based on population density data from the Federal Highway Administration and trip distance data from the Census of Population and Housing. Other economic variables are from Department of Transportation, Section 15 database. Data on the policymaking entities are from a Brookings Institution survey in conjunction with the National Association of Regional Councils. Data on constituents are from the Census of Population and Housing.

a. White heteroskedastic standard errors in parentheses.

policymaking entities, and constituents are distinguished from economic variables because of their inconsistency with achieving economic efficiency. In what follows, we first report the parameter estimates for each attribute equation and then summarize our findings for bus service.[11]

Fare Equation

We found that the economic variables had their expected effects: greater trip distances, vehicle capacities, operating expenses, and population densities raise average bus fares, and greater route densities lower them. We also found that fares decrease as an urbanized area increases its reliance on

11. It may be tempting to provide quantitative interpretations of parameter estimates for individual equations. But it is important to bear in mind that because we are analyzing a system of equations, it is not appropriate to draw quantitative conclusions without simulating, where appropriate, a variable's effect on all the attributes. This will be done after we describe our qualitative findings.

purchased and private bus transportation, although the effect of the private buses is statistically weak.[12] Finally, government subsidies appear to provide some benefits to travelers because they lower average fares.

The estimates also show that bus fares can be affected by the entity responsible for setting fares.[13] All else constant, average fares are lower when a city makes these decisions. But governors can have an indirect influence because fares are also lower when a governor-appointed transit authority makes the decisions. Fares are also affected by bus transportation constituencies. All else constant, average bus fares fall as the share of young and Asian-American bus riders in the commuting population increases, but rise as the share of middle-income bus riders in the commuting population increases.[14]

Route Coverage Equation

As expected, route coverage is increased by greater population densities, but other standard economic variables tend to have statistically insignificant

12. One might question the direction of causality and argue that the presence of purchased and private bus transportation is influenced by the level of fares. As we noted in chapter 2, because all bus systems' fares are set by a public policymaking entity, private systems can only offer suggestions and ideas relevant to fare decisions. It is therefore unlikely that an urbanized area's fares influence private or purchased systems to serve the area because these systems do not have independent authority to change fares.

13. It might be argued that the policymaking entities are endogenous, that is, the entity is determined by a particular type of system. We pointed out in chapter 2, however, that previous researchers have not offered a systematic reason why a particular entity bears responsibility for fare and route coverage decisions in a given area. We developed a multinomial logit model that attempted to explain the policymaking entity as a function of an area's economic and demographic characteristics but found that this model had little explanatory power.

14. Bus transportation constituents are defined as a percentage of the eligible voters in an urbanized area. We explored other specifications for these constituents (as a percentage of all work trip bus travelers, for instance) but the specifications produced less satisfactory statistical fits. It could be argued that defining bus constituencies in terms of bus travelers leads to endogeneity problems (for example, the share of middle-income bus riders in the eligible voting population might be affected by bus fares). As an alternative, we defined constituencies in terms of *travelers* (the share of middle-income travelers in the eligible voting population), which would be a truly exogenous measure. We found, however, that this specification of constituents did not affect our findings. Finally, it might be argued that our findings simply reflect the fact that certain groups of travelers live in urbanized areas that have bus systems with relatively higher or lower fares. Although this may be true in isolated instances, it is not likely that the residential location of socioeconomic groups is systematically correlated with transit attributes (middle-class bus travelers, for example, are not likely inherently to live in areas with higher bus fares).

effects. Route coverage shrinks as the share of bus miles provided by purchased transportation or private operators increases. It also decreases when local entities make route coverage decisions and when they are the recipients of federal mass transportation funds. It increases when governors make the decisions.

As with fares, route coverage is affected by the characteristics of bus users. Increases in the share of lower-income and upper middle-income bus users expand route coverage. But, holding users' income and other influences constant, route coverage contracts as the percentage of black and Hispanic bus users rises.[15]

Service Frequency Equation

Economic considerations apparently are more important in determining frequency of service than in determining route coverage. Population density increases frequency, while greater operating expenses and route coverage decrease it.[16] An expanded share of bus service by either purchased transportation or private operators leads to greater frequency. Government subsidies also increase frequency.

Nearly all the policymaking entities have distinct effects on service frequency. Governors with the authority to make route coverage decisions promote frequency, as do governor-appointed and popularly elected transit authorities and local entities such as a mayor's office. Bus frequency also increases as the share of lower-income and lower middle-income riders expands, but decreases as the share of upper middle-income riders expands. Finally, bus frequency increases as the share of Asian-American riders increases.

15. This finding is broadly consistent with some anecdotal evidence reported in the press, which describes communities rallying against extensions to their transit systems because of fears that these extensions will lead to an increase in crime. Again, one might argue that blacks and Hispanics live in areas that happen to have less route coverage. But this explanation seems unlikely in our context because ethnic minorities tend to live in more densely populated areas and, as we reported, greater population densities increase route coverage.

16. It might be expected that fares would affect demand, which in turn would affect frequency. We found, however, that fares had a statistically insignificant effect on frequency. Apparently, population density rather than demand per se influences frequency.

Summary

The central theme of our findings is that economic variables fall short of explaining bus pricing and service policy. Notwithstanding our qualification that the current state of theory and empirical evidence prevented us from fully justifying why we found that certain political variables were influential and others were not, it is clear that politics, in general, has influenced policy on bus transportation and thus emerged as the likely source of the inefficient policies that we have identified.

To be sure, conventional economic considerations do help determine transit attributes, and their effects are generally plausible. Urban areas with greater population densities have systems with greater route coverage and frequency and higher fares. Those areas with higher operating costs have bus systems that charge higher fares and offer less frequent service. Private and purchased bus operators differ from traditional public companies in providing more frequent bus service with less route coverage and lower fares.[17]

The effects of the political influences are also plausible. Government subsidies are used in part to lower fares and increase frequency. And some policymaking entities appear to encourage the development of a particular type of bus system. Governors promote systems with greater route coverage and service frequency while their appointed transit authorities keep fares low. Local entities tend to promote systems with less route coverage, lower fares, and greater frequency. This finding is consistent with the view that the farther the political management of transit systems is from the locality served, the greater the pressures to expand route coverage to outlying areas so that suburban residents can be assessed part of the transit deficit (usually in the form of higher property taxes).

17. Roger F. Teal, "Public Transit Service Contracting: A Status Report," *Transportation Quarterly*, vol. 42 (April 1988), pp. 207–22, finds that contracting with private transit providers can reduce costs and subsidies by 10 to 50 percent. The simple comparison in chapter 2 between public and private bus carriers also indicated that private carriers provided greater frequency (but reduced coverage) and required less subsidy than public carriers. But private carriers' average fares in this comparison were higher than public carriers' fares (private carriers' effect on fares in the bus fare equation was actually statistically insignificant). This difference could have arisen because the simple comparison between public and private carriers only included urban areas that were served solely by private or public bus carriers, while the bus fare equation included urban areas that were served by public and private bus carriers.

Finally, particular socioeconomic groups may accrue benefits, which to some extent are shared by other socioeconomic groups, because of their political influence or as a by-product of policymakers' common goals. Political influence seems consistent with falling fares and increased frequency as the share of Asian-American bus riders expands. We can only speculate that Asian-Americans' distinct statistical influence accords with their greater preference than other travelers for public transit.[18] That benefits accrue as a by-product of policymakers' common goals seems consistent with declining bus fares as the share of young bus riders increases, and with bus frequency and route coverage increasing as the share of lower-income bus riders increases. The finding that route coverage shrinks as the share of black and Hispanic bus riders increases probably reflects these groups' lack of political influence on urban bus policy. The effects of middle-income bus riders on bus attributes appear to reflect a combination of political influence and policymakers' common goals. An increase in the share of upper middle-income riders leads to greater route coverage but less frequency, which may reflect these riders' preference for a system that improves accessibility, even at some cost to convenience. Service frequency increases as the share of the lower middle-income bus riding population expands, but fares rise as the share of the middle-income bus riding population expands.

Specification and Estimation of Rail Attributes

We used the same framework to analyze the determinants of rail attributes as we did to analyze the determinants of bus attributes. Rail fares, route coverage, and frequency of service were assumed to be influenced by the economic characteristics of the system and its operating environment. They were also assumed to be influenced by government subsidies, the policymaking entity, and rail constituents. As

18. We investigated whether Asian-Americans' influence was a proxy for such factors as a western or more specifically a California location, a location in a small (or large) city, or a Honolulu effect. Dummy variables for western, California, and small-city locations were statistically insignificant and had no effect on the Asian-American coefficient. Removing Honolulu from the sample also had no effect on the Asian-American coefficient.

before, preliminary estimation revealed that some of these variables had a statistically significant effect on some attributes but not on others. Thus we generally eliminated the highly insignificant variables from the appropriate equations when we estimated our system of rail attribute equations.[19] We summarize our findings for rail transit in the text and report and describe the specific parameter estimates of the attribute equations in appendix C.

Urban areas with greater population densities have rail systems with greater route coverage, more frequent service, and higher fares. Government subsidies benefit all urban rail systems by supporting lower fares and more frequent service. These findings are consistent with the effects of economic factors and subsidies on urban bus systems.

Bus and rail systems are affected somewhat differently by policymakers and transportation constituents. Mayors or other city officials may value the prestige that accompanies a major urban rail system, but unless they directly receive federal grant money, they tend to favor higher fares and less frequency. Governor-appointed transit authorities try to create smaller systems with more frequent service. The lack of strong support for rail by any policymaking entity is consistent with some evidence that these systems have little effect on employment or land use in station areas and thus cannot be depended on to generate political support from the business community.[20] In addition, state and local governments may be less supportive of rail systems than they are of bus systems (unless they receive a large commitment of federal funds) because they would bear fiscal responsibility for maintaining a costly underused rail system if abandonment is not an option. In some states, gasoline tax revenues cannot be used to provide matching funds for transit projects, which means that policymakers must embark on the politically unpleasant mission of obtaining money from other sources. For example, state and local governments in the Washington, D.C., metropolitan area recently raised concerns about where

19. In a few instances we report a statistically imprecise coefficient for a variable if that finding per se is of particular interest.

20. See Christopher R. Bollinger and Keith R. Ihlanfeldt, "The Impact of Rapid Rail Transit on Economic Development: The Case of Atlanta's MARTA," *Journal of Urban Economics*, vol. 42 (September 1997), pp. 179–204.

they would obtain $100 million a year to fund Metrorail's maintenance needs for the next decade.[21]

Rail systems are clearly responsive to the interests of upper middle-income riders because fares fall and route coverage and frequency increase as their share of ridership increases.[22] In contrast, fares increase and service frequency deteriorates as the share of (lower) middle-income riders increases, and route coverage contracts as the share of lower-income riders increases.[23]

Sources of the Welfare Loss from Transit

The preceding estimation results identify the primary political sources of the welfare loss from inefficient transit pricing and service. As we showed in chapter 4, although economic efficiency generally requires higher transit fares and less frequent service, government subsidies lead to lower fares and more frequent service.[24] Policymaking entities also pursue objectives that conflict with efficiency. Governors, either directly or through their appointed transit authorities, encourage larger bus systems that, all else constant, offer greater frequency and lower fares. Local entities encourage smaller bus systems, but they too encourage greater frequencies and lower fares. Although the policymakers' objectives appear to conflict less often

21. Alice Reid, "Region Faces Big Bill for Metro's Upkeep," *Washington Post*, April 9, 1998, p. D7. Similar concerns may be motivating some Los Angeles public officials to call for a stop to building any more of the city's new rail system. See William Claiborne, "L.A. Subway Tests Mass Transit Limits," *Washington Post*, June 10, 1998, p. A1.

22. This finding is partially corroborated by Robert Cooter and Gregory Topakian, "Political Economy of a Public Corporation: Pricing Objectives of BART," *Journal of Public Economics*, vol. 13 (June 1980), pp. 299–318, who find that BART's fare structure benefits wealthier people who commute from the suburbs.

23. Edward Walsh, "Highway Bill Could Help, Hurt Atlanta," *Washington Post*, April 12, 1998, p. A4, reports that in response to the uneven development of Atlanta's MARTA system, the president of the Metro Atlanta Chamber of Commerce cited suburban fears that a rail link to the inner city would bring inner-city problems to their communities.

24. From a second-best perspective, a variable may increase efficiency by offsetting the effect of other variables. For example, certain influences may raise fares above marginal cost, while government subsidies offset this effect by reducing fares below marginal cost. Nonetheless, from a first-best perspective, subsidies contribute to pricing distortions.

with efficiency in rail transportation, there too some inefficiencies appear (frequency of service increases under the authority of governor-appointed transit agencies). Finally, inefficiencies arise in accordance with the socio-economic groups who use transit—bus fares fall or frequency increases or both as the share of young, lower-income, lower middle-income, and Asian-American bus riders grows, while rail fares fall and frequency increases as the share of upper middle-income rail users increases.

We now quantify the contribution that government subsidies, policy-making entities, and constituents have made to the loss of social welfare from inefficient transit pricing and service.[25] Our primary objective is not to itemize the impact of these factors—which are arguably interdependent—but to document empirically the full influence of politics on urban transportation efficiency and to assess the implications of this influence on the potential for policymakers to improve urban transit.

We first assessed the attribute equations' prediction capabilities by re-estimating the net benefits from optimal transit prices and service frequency using the prices and frequencies predicted by the attribute equations instead of the actual prices and frequencies.[26] The estimated net benefits are within $100 million, or 2 percent, of the net benefits from using actual prices and frequencies, indicating a small prediction error.

We quantified the welfare loss from each source by predicting prices and frequencies after eliminating the effect of a particular variable or set of variables from the attribute equations.[27] The resulting predicted prices and frequencies replaced the prices and frequencies that were predicted by attribute equations that included the effects of all relevant variables. A variable's contribution to the welfare loss is the *difference* between the welfare loss when we accounted for a variable's influence on prices and frequencies

25. In chapter 4 we reported that inefficient transit operating practices were responsible for a $0.7 billion reduction in economic welfare and that government subsidies were the prime source of these inefficiencies. There are undoubtedly other sources.

26. Although our welfare analysis will focus on fares and frequencies, in the full system of simultaneous equations any changes in route coverage resulting from a change in an exogenous variable will affect all of the attributes. Thus our simulations account for the effects of changes in route coverage on fares and service frequency.

27. This was accomplished by setting the variable, or effectively the impact of the variable (its parameter), to equal zero.

Table 5-2. *Sources of Welfare Loss from Transit Operations*

Percent unless otherwise specified

| Influence that is eliminated | Change in bus | | Change in rail | | Welfare improvement (millions of dollars) |
	Fare	Frequency	Fare	Frequency	
Subsidies	15.7	−15.3	12.4	−36.1	1,460
Local decisionmaking entities	23.0	−18.0	−8.4	30.8	190
Governor-appointed transit authorities	2.7	−3.6	−0.8	−12.3	580
Constitiuents (socioeconomic and ethnic groups)	3.7	−29.6	−0.2	29.0	3,770

Source: Authors' calculations.

and the welfare loss when it was assumed that the variable did not have an influence on prices and frequencies.[28]

The results of these calculations are presented in table 5-2. The effect of government subsidies has been to cause bus and rail fares to be lower and service more frequent than optimal. The table shows that eliminating the subsidies would sharply raise prices and reduce frequency, closing the $7.4 billion welfare loss from inefficient pricing and service by $1.5 billion. Given that operating subsidies in 1990 were $9.2 billion, the return that these subsidies provided to travelers is actually small, which accords with the findings of other researchers, who conclude that the primary beneficiaries of federal subsidies are not travelers but transit operators and the suppliers of transit labor and capital.[29]

Some policymaking entities' pricing and service decisions may deviate from economic efficiency to achieve a redistributive goal. Thus it is important

28. We assumed that other factors remain constant when we eliminated the effect of a particular variable or set of variables. It is difficult to assess how, if at all, other variables would change in response to eliminating the effect of any of the political factors. Thus the welfare loss attributable to subsidies, for example, is obtained by assuming that subsidies are eliminated and that other variables do not change in response.

29. See Don H. Pickrell, "Rising Deficits and the Uses of Transit Subsidies in the United States," *Journal of Transport Economics and Policy*, vol. 19 (September 1985), pp. 281–98; and Douglass B. Lee, *Evaluation of Federal Transit Operating Subsidies* (Transportation Systems Center, Department of Transportation, 1987).

to assess the redistributive consequences of efficient urban transportation policy, which we will do shortly. In the meantime, our findings indicate that distortions in transit prices and frequency created by policymaking entities turn out to account for a modest part of the welfare loss. Local entities have caused lower than optimal bus fares and higher than optimal frequencies of service. Although they have partly offset these distortions by raising rail fares and reducing rail service frequencies, their contribution to welfare loss comes to nearly $200 million. Governor-appointed transit authorities cause greater than optimal rail and bus frequencies, which creates an additional $580 million in welfare costs. Collectively, these policymaking entities account for $780 million of the welfare loss from transit operations.[30]

We have argued that because urban transportation prices and service are regulated and because these regulations have contributed to serious inefficiencies, it is unlikely that prices and service have been adjusted in response to the socioeconomic composition of an urbanized area's bus and rail travelers to improve efficiency. Indeed, the welfare loss is reduced by $3.8 billion if the influence of these transportation constituencies on fares and frequencies is eliminated. The source of the improvement, however, is surprising. Constituency influence has, on net, caused bus fares to be somewhat lower than optimal and rail fares to be slightly *higher* than optimal, and it has caused rail service to be less frequent than optimal. The conflicting effects of various constituents have thus sometimes led to transit attributes that are actually unfavorable to travelers as a whole. A greater presence of lower-income and lower middle-income riders has raised the frequency of bus service above optimal levels. Eliminating this influence would reduce bus frequency and greatly reduce the welfare loss associated with transit users.

30. It would be misleading to conclude from this exercise that welfare would necessarily be improved if decisionmaking authority were transferred from local entities and governor-appointed transit authorities to some other entities. That is, the welfare estimates were obtained by using our estimate of an entity's effect on fares and service when it has decisionmaking authority and by assuming that, all else constant, the policymaking entity has no distinct impact on fares and service (that is, its estimated coefficients are set to zero). We cannot infer from this approach what would happen to fares and service if decisionmaking authority were transferred to another entity. One could, in principle, use our model to estimate what would happen if, for example, all fare decisions were made by the governor. The difficulty with this calculation is that it would assume that the governor's effect on fares in a few urban areas is the same as it would be in all the urban areas in our sample.

We can thus attribute more than 80 percent of the welfare loss from sub-optimal urban transit fares and frequencies to well-defined political influences.[31] (In appendix D, we show that this conclusion is not altered when we use attribute equations that are estimated by simpler econometric methods.)[32] Although there are undoubtedly important political influences that we have not accounted for, it is clear that the inefficiencies in urban transit pricing and service cannot be explained by some "mistake" that can be easily corrected. The inefficiencies are caused by entrenched political forces, a situation that must be borne in mind when we consider how to improve the efficiency of the U.S. urban transit system.

Sources of Inefficiencies in Automobile Travel

We have found that the failure to price automobile transportation efficiently does *not* lend legitimacy to subsidizing transit (and vice versa), but we have also estimated that more than one-third of the welfare gains from an urban transportation policy based on net-benefit maximization would come from setting efficient automobile congestion tolls. Tolls that vary by time of day, in accordance with traffic volumes and road capacities, would represent a major departure from current road pricing, which is primarily based on the gasoline tax. Unfortunately, it is difficult to investigate directly why current pricing deviates from optimal congestion tolls. In particular, it does not seem possible to establish empirically a link between automobile pricing and the sorts of political factors that we found to influence transit attributes.

Previous research, however, has appeared to reach a consensus about why congestion tolls have not been implemented. The basic argument is that the tolls would benefit only a minority of (generally wealthy) travelers,

31. We found that transportation constituents account for $3.77 billion of the loss, subsidies for $1.46 billion, and policymaking entities for $0.78 billion for a total of $6.1 billion, which is 81 percent of the $7.4 billion welfare loss from suboptimal transit fares and service frequencies that we estimated in table 4-1.

32. Appendix D presents welfare loss calculations based on (single-equation) generalized least squares estimates of the attribute equations instead of three-stage least squares estimates. This sensitivity analysis is important because simultaneous equations parameter estimates can be "contaminated" by specification errors in one of the equations.

whose value of the travel time savings would exceed the out-of-pocket costs of the toll.[33] In other words, highway constituents, like transit constituents, have conflicting interests that ultimately discourage efficient road pricing. John Calfee and Clifford Winston take this explanation further.[34] They find that automobile travelers' willingness to pay to save travel time by having road authorities set congestion tolls on highways is much weaker than implied by previous estimates, and conclude that even wealthy automobile travelers do not appear to value travel time savings enough to benefit substantially from optimal tolls.[35] They also find that automobile travelers' willingness to pay is insensitive to how the toll revenue is disbursed, a concern thought by some to be instrumental in the public's resistance to congestion pricing.

Policy entities that have goals that are at variance with transportation efficiency, and politically influential (or targeted) interest groups that are able to accrue benefits at the expense of society could also undermine the implementation of congestion tolls. The recent failure to impose these tolls on the San Francisco Bay Bridge is illustrative. Stephen Shmanske points out that as part of a congressionally approved congestion pricing demonstration project, the Metropolitan Transportation Commission and the California Department of Transportation approved a toll increase during morning and afternoon rush hours. According to their plan, the toll revenues were to be redistributed among various public agencies overseeing alternative transit modes (some funds were to go toward a discount for eligible lower-income commuters). The state legislature interpreted this plan

33. See, for example, Steven A. Morrison, "A Survey of Road Pricing," *Transportation Research*, vol. 20A (March 1986), pp. 89–97; and Kenneth A. Small and José A. Gomez-Ibañez, "Urban Transportation," in Paul Cheshire and Edwin S. Mills, eds., *Handbook of Regional and Urban Economics*, vol. 3: *Applied Urban Economics* (Amsterdam: North-Holland, forthcoming).

34. John Calfee and Clifford Winston, "The Value of Automobile Travel Time: Implications for Congestion Policy," *Journal of Public Economics*, vol. 69 (July 1998), pp. 83–102.

35. Calfee and Winston, "Value of Automobile Travel Time," find that travelers' value of automobile travel time as a fraction of their wage is closer to 20 percent, as compared with the "consensus" value of 50 percent. The difference arises because the consensus estimate is based on mode choice models that include the disutility of time spent on alternative modes such as transit, which raises the value of travel time. This effect is not captured in Calfee and Winston's stated preference analysis of how much *automobile* travelers are willing to pay to reduce travel time.

as essentially a tax increase designed to redistribute funds to bureaucratically controlled, loss-making transit systems and flatly rejected it.[36]

Policymakers' primary method of combating congestion has been to build more roads. But as funds for additional roads have become harder to come by, many urban officials have confined their activities to "studying" ways to reduce congestion.[37] Americans may have to look beyond the public sector if major pricing experiments to relieve highway congestion are ever to be initiated.

Conclusion

It is no accident that the U.S. urban transportation system is riddled with inefficiencies. In principle, the public policies controlling the system are vulnerable to political influences. In practice, government subsidies, competing objectives of policy entities, and the benefits and costs conferred on various transportation constituencies account for most of the welfare loss in transit, although it is difficult to assess their role in explaining the welfare costs in automobile transportation.

One might attempt to justify these inefficiencies by arguing that they are the price for a uniformly laudable redistribution of income. But the inefficiencies are not purposeful or targeted. Instead, everyone gets something and the taxpayers ultimately foot the bill. Thus lower-income and lower middle-income bus riders encourage more frequent service, while upper middle-income rail riders encourage more frequent service and greater system coverage, and so on. (Recall from chapter 1 that public

36. Stephen Shmanske, "The Bay Bridge Blunder," *Regulation*, vol. 19, no. 4 (1996), pp. 58–64. The state legislature did not suggest how the plan could be salvaged.

37. For example, the Los Angeles Board of Airport Commissioners awarded a $458,582 contract for a study on ways to reduce congestion at the Los Angeles airport; see "Study on Reducing Airport Traffic Okd," *Los Angeles Times,* October 22, 1997. The Greater Washington Board of Trade undertook a $350,000 study of ways to head off increasing congestion in the Washington, D.C., area. The Board of Trade concluded that political obstacles would seem to put a regionwide strategy out of reach. See Peter Behr, "Area Leaders Hit Traffic Roadblock: Political Obstacles Hamper Solutions to Driving Woes," *Washington Post,* September 28, 1997, p. A1.

funds are subsidizing bus commuters, whose average household income in 1995 was $40,000 and rail commuters, whose average income was at least $50,000.) It may be believed that transit is designed to help the elderly and the poor, but it is far from clear that these people are transit's greatest beneficiaries.[38]

38. In Los Angeles, a class action suit was filed in 1994 charging that the Metropolitan Transportation Authority operates separate and unequal bus and rail systems and discriminates against poor minority bus riders. The suit was precipitated by MTA's attempt to raise fares and eliminate the monthly pass. In 1996 a consent decree settled the suit, with fares maintained and the bus pass kept. Martin Kasindorf, "L.A. Spinning its Wheels over Transit Plan," *USA Today*, July 3, 1997, p. 14A, points out that some communities and policymakers continue to resist allocating funds for rail service to low-income areas of East Los Angeles. Generally, Mahlon R. Straszheim, "Assessing the Social Costs of Urban Transportation Technologies," in Peter Mieszkowski and Marlon Straszheim, eds., *Current Issues in Urban Transportation* (Johns Hopkins University Press, 1979), pp. 196–232, and Alan Hay, "Equity and Welfare in the Geography of Public Transport Provision," *Journal of Transport Geography*, vol. 6 (1993), pp. 95–101, argue that the tax burden for transit takes a larger portion of income from the poor than it does from the rich.

6

An Alternative Route: Privatization

WHEN EVALUATING a public policy, economists normally begin by asking whether it maximizes economic efficiency. That benchmark is arguably inappropriate when the policy has a goal apart from economic efficiency, although even then it can usefully be asked whether the particular goal is being achieved at the least possible cost to society.

As is evident from our demonstration of the potentially large net benefits available to society from an urban transportation policy that sets prices and service frequencies efficiently and promotes efficient operations, today's urban transportation policy is assuredly *not* directed at achieving maximum efficiency, nor does it seem to keep accident costs or pollution to a minimum. Policymakers at all levels of government have shaped an urban transportation system that benefits various travelers and suppliers, but whose welfare costs are borne by all taxpayers.[1] And as long as transit prices and service are determined by the public sector, it is hard to see how the current welfare costs—primarily caused by government subsidies, policy entities, and transportation constituents—could be significantly reduced. Indeed, federal transit policy for the next several years, as encapsulated in the

---

1. We have reported evidence that the primary beneficiaries of federal subsidies are transit operators and the suppliers of transit labor and capital. In addition, Kenneth M. Chomitz and Charles A. Lave, "Part-Time Labor, Work Rules, and Urban Transit Costs," *Journal of Transport Economics and Policy*, vol. 18 (January 1984), pp. 63–73, and Jean Love and Wendell Cox, "False Dreams and Broken Promises: The Wasteful Federal Investment in Urban Mass Transit," policy analysis 162, Cato Institute,Washington, 1991, point out that transit agencies in particular effectively serve the interests of transit unions when planning services and route structures. Because subsidies generally attract rent seekers, it is likely that consultants, planners, economists, and so on have also benefited from them.

Transportation Equity Act for the 21st Century discussed in chapter 1, indicates that there will be no serious break with past policy.

There is, however, an alternative that merits serious consideration. Urban transit efficiency *could* be improved if it were shielded from political influences and exposed to competitive forces through some form of privatization.[2] In this chapter, we provide rough estimates of the economic effects of privatizing transit and discuss the practical issues involved in implementing this policy. We then briefly consider the role of private roads in automobile travel and how taxi operations would be affected by deregulation.

We do not view privatization (and deregulation) as ends in themselves. Rather, their compelling feature is that they represent an effective way—perhaps the only realistic way—to stimulate competition in all modes of urban transportation, competition that would mostly eliminate the huge inefficiencies that have developed under public sector management. In addition, we contend that opponents of privatization, like opponents of economic deregulation, vastly overstate the potential for this policy to benefit the wealthy citizens at the expense of the poor, and that like economic deregulation, many of privatization's distributional effects are likely to be surprisingly favorable.

Privatization of Urban Transit

We obtained estimates of the economic effects of privatizing transit by calculating the changes in the welfare of travelers, bus and rail companies, and taxpayers that would result from having prices and service determined by private bus and rail companies instead of the public sector. We converted our net-benefit maximization model into a privatization model by making

2. Several authors have discussed the effects of privatizing urban transit. See, among others, Charles A. Lave, ed., *Urban Transit: The Private Challenge to Public Transportation* (Cambridge, Mass.: Ballinger, 1985); Robert W. Poole Jr. and Philip E. Fixler Jr., "Privatization of Public-Sector Services in Practice: Experience and Potential," *Journal of Policy Analysis and Management*, vol. 6 (Summer 1987), pp. 612–25; and José A. Gomez-Ibañez and John R. Meyer, *Going Private: The International Experience with Transport Privatization* (Brookings, 1993). Gabriel Roth, *Roads in a Market Economy* (Aldershot, England: Avebury Technical, 1996), assesses the consequences of privatizing highways.

some plausible assumptions regarding the competitive behavior of private bus and rail firms. First, using a modeling framework developed by Philip Viton, we assumed each bus and rail company would behave in a Cournot-like fashion by taking the prices and service qualities of the other companies as given while setting its own prices and service to maximize profit.[3] Second, we have pointed out that public transit companies operate inefficiently and that their marginal costs would be reduced at least 15 percent if they were more efficient. Bus and rail companies would likely become more efficient if they were privatized because they would have greater incentives and operating freedom to optimize their use of labor and equipment and to adopt the latest technologies to improve routing, scheduling, and pricing. As a conservative base case assumption, we reduced the marginal costs of private bus and rail companies 25 percent from their current levels and increased bus and rail's average load factor to 50 percent (recall, public buses' average load factor is 14.3 percent and rail's is 17.6 percent.)[4] Finally, in our base case we assumed that no new transit organization would enter the market, but we later relaxed this assumption.

Equilibrium in our urban areas was achieved by (iterative) maximization of bus and rail profit and (iterative) maximization of net benefits from

3. Philip A. Viton, "On Competition and Product Differentiation in Urban Transportation: The San Francisco Bay Area," *Bell Journal of Economics*, vol. 12 (Autumn 1981), pp. 362–79. In a perfectly competitive environment, maximizing profit is equivalent to maximizing net benefits. We are not assuming, however, that urban transportation would be perfectly competitive.

4. Our estimate of the reduction in marginal costs from privatizing transit is conservative compared with that of Charles Lave, "Measuring the Decline in Transit Productivity in the U.S.," *Transportation Planning and Technology*, vol. 15, no. 2/4 (1991), pp. 115–24. Lave finds that transit productivity has declined 40 percent since the public takeovers in the mid-1960s and the subsequent subsidies of what had been a privately owned transit industry (p. 115). In addition, Gomez-Ibañez and Meyer, *Going Private*, found that costs fall an average 31 percent when private contractors substitute for public agencies on fixed bus routes (p. 68). Recent anecdotal evidence also points out that it costs public agencies much more than private companies to provide bus service. Alice Reid, "Metrobus's Future Is Topic of Summit," *Washington Post*, January 5, 1997, p. B4, reports that public officials in Falls Church, Virginia, claimed that a private contractor could provide comparable service at 60 percent less than the (public) Metro costs the city. In "Bumpy Road Ahead for Metrobus Plan," *Washington Post*, August 24, 1997, p. B1, Reid reports that the typical Metrobus driver gets paid as much as 50 percent more than drivers for private bus companies in the Washington area. It is also reasonable to assume that private transit systems would operate with average load factors of at least 50 percent. Indeed, commercial airlines achieve average load factors of 55 percent on routes that are composed of the smallest airports in the country (nonhubs).

Table 6-1. *Comparison of Net Benefits from Privatization and Net-Benefit Maximization of Bus and Rail Operations under Alternative Assumptions*

Billions of 1990 dollars

Assumptions	Consumer benefits	Government balances and carrier profits	Net benefits
Bus and rail privatization (profit maximization with market entry restrictions), with marginal costs of transit reduced 15 percent and optimal auto tolls	−14.1	24.9	10.8
Price and service optimization of bus and rail (marginal cost pricing and optimal transit service frequency), with marginal costs of transit reduced 15 percent and optimal auto tolls	−13.3	24.8	11.5
Bus and rail privatization, with optimal auto toll and marginal costs of transit reduced 25 percent and average load factors raised to 50 percent	−13.2	25.4	12.2
Bus and rail privatization, with optimal auto tolls and marginal costs of transit reduced 35 percent and average load factors raised to 60 percent	−13.0	25.7	12.7
Price and service optimization of bus and rail, with marginal costs of transit reduced 35 percent and average load factors raised to 60 percent and optimal auto tolls	−11.6	25.5	13.9

Source: Authors' calculations. Negative sign indicates loss in benefits.

an optimal congestion toll.[5] Table 6-1 presents estimates of the net social benefits from the privatization of bus and rail operations and compares them with the estimated net benefits from optimal pricing and service frequency under public management that were presented in chapter 4, assuming that the marginal costs of transit in both environments are reduced 15 percent from current levels. The economic effects of privatization and those of net-benefit maximization are remarkably similar. Compared with net-benefit maximization, travelers experience a somewhat greater loss in

5. Equilibrium is reached when no transit company has an incentive to change its price and service, given the prices and service of the other companies. To obtain aggregate estimates for all trips, we have assumed in previous simulations that nonwork trips had 50 percent of the value of work trips. We have maintained that assumption in this simulation. Finally, our aggregate modal choice parameters were based on travelers' behavior with public urban transportation. Because we have not been able to determine how these parameters might change, if at all, if public transit were privatized, we have qualified our findings by noting that we assumed modal choice parameters were not affected by privatization.

welfare under privatization, while government balances and bus and rail profits are slightly higher.[6] The annual net benefits from privatization and optimal congestion tolls are only $0.7 billion short of the net benefits from optimal pricing and service of publicly managed transit and optimal congestion tolls.

We noted earlier, however, that transit companies would become more efficient under private management than they would be under public management. When we employed our base case private sector assumptions (marginal costs of transit operations are reduced 25 percent from their current levels and load factors rise to 50 percent), the annual net benefits from privatization and optimal congestion tolls rise to $12.2 billion, which exceeds the gain from net-benefit maximization in the public sector. If transit operations become more efficient than we assumed (for example, marginal costs fall 35 percent and load factors increase to 60 percent), net benefits increase another $0.5 billion to $12.7 billion. And these benefits are achieved without considering the effect of new operators entering the market. If new market entry led to competition that was sufficiently intense to generate socially optimal pricing and service, annual net benefits would approach $14 billion.

Although benefits under privatization are characterized by increases in transit fares and decreases in service frequency, the costs to travelers are steadily reduced as competition becomes more intense (that is, generates marginal cost pricing; see table 6-2). To be sure, it is unlikely that private transit markets will become perfectly competitive, but even a rail transit monopoly would face strong competition from private bus companies, taxis, and autos. And because some public rail systems were constructed when it would have been more efficient for bus companies to serve travelers, it is likely that in a privatized urban transit system some rail operations will be abandoned or substantially cut back and replaced by bus

6. The average annual bus company profit under privatization is estimated to be $453,000, compared with $177,000 under net-benefit maximization. The average annual rail operations profit under privatization is estimated to be $21 million, compared with $14 million under net-benefit maximization. Philip A. Viton, "The Possibility of Profitable Bus Service," *Journal of Transport Economics and Policy*, vol. 14 (September 1980), pp. 295–314, also finds that privatized bus service can be profitable.

Table 6-2. *Transit Mode Shares and Attributes under Privatization and Net Benefit Maximization*[a]

Attributes	Initial value	Private value	Socially optimal value
Transit fares (cents per mile)			
Bus	13.2	37.6	27.7
Rail	17.4	35.5	21.6
Transit frequencies (number of times a route mile is covered per hour)			
Bus	0.95	0.23	0.30
Rail	20.80	4.88	5.88
Mode share (percent)			
Auto	79.1	81.4	80.4
Car pool	14.3	15.5	15.3
Bus	4.7	1.7	2.6
Rail	1.1	0.5	0.9
Taxi	0.8	0.8	0.8

Source: Authors' calculations.
a. Assumes marginal costs of transit reduced 35 percent and average load factors raised to 60 percent.

operations.[7] Finally, greater efficiency and competition can slow the shrinkage of transit's mode share.

As transit companies adjust to a competitive environment, the benefits from privatization, especially for travelers, are likely to grow. Retrospective evaluations of the effects of economic deregulation have repeatedly found that industries that are no longer subject to regulations that inhibit techno- logical innovations have greatly improved their cost efficiency and service to customers.[8] Transit is likely to benefit from new technologies that are currently being suppressed by regulation, such as personal rapid transit (PRT), real-time demand-responsive communications, and others that are likely to occur in a fully competitive environment but are often difficult to

7. José A. Gomez-Ibañez, "A Dark Side to Light Rail?" *Journal of the American Planning Association*, vol. 51 (Summer 1985), pp. 337–51, and John F. Kain, "Cost-Effective Alternatives to Atlanta's Rail Rapid Transit System," *Journal of Transport Economics and Policy*, vol. 31 (January 1997), pp. 25–50, identify specific cases where it would have been more cost effective to use busses instead of rail to provide mass transit.

8. See Clifford Winston, "U.S. Industry Adjustment to Economic Deregulation," *Journal of Economic Perspectives*, vol. 12 (Summer 1998).

predict.[9] The deregulation experience has also taught us that new market entrants have often become the most efficient firms in a deregulated industry and a primary source of greater competition, which leads to lower prices for consumers.[10] In the transit industry, privatization could lead to intense competition supplied by paratransit operations, such as jitneys, and more conventional low-cost operations, such as minibuses.[11] Indeed, many travelers in New York City have found that the fares and service offered by illegal gypsy vans are preferable to the fares and service offered by public transit.[12] Even conventional transit companies using current technologies will be more responsive to travelers than public agencies are now. They will have the incentive and freedom to adjust their networks to changes in employment opportunities and demographics and to develop pricing and service innovations, such as fine-tuned peak and off-peak pricing and well-coordinated intermodal operations.

As they have with intercity transportation, urban travelers will seek to minimize cost increases in a privatized transit market by adjusting their travel behavior and developing bargaining power with private transit operators. These considerations suggest that in the long run travelers are likely to see from privatization much smaller fare increases than our model predicts and possibly an overall improvement in service.[13]

9. Andy Newman, "M.T.A. Seeks to Automate Subway Lines," *New York Times*, October 27, 1997, p. B1, points out that much of the present system for signaling and controlling New York City subway trains dates back to the turn of the century. A more automated system is expected to take twenty years to put in place.

10. The emergence of Southwest Airlines as a competitive force for low fares following airline deregulation is a good example of this phenomenon.

11. Robert Cervero, *Paratransit in America: Redefining Mass Transportation* (Praeger, 1997), points out that paratransit operations, including jitneys and vans, have lower operating costs per passenger mile than current bus and rail operations. Paratransit's cost advantage comes from higher load factors and lower labor costs. Daniel B. Klein, Adrian T. Moore, and Binyam Reja, *Curb Rights: A Foundation for Free Enterprise in Urban Transit* (Brookings, 1997), point out that jitneys have had limited success in the past because they have had to compete with subsidized bus companies.

12. John Tierney, "Man with a Van," *New York Times Magazine*, August 10, 1997, p. 22.

13. Clifford Winston, "Economic Deregulation: Days of Reckoning for Microeconomists," *Journal of Economic Literature*, vol. 31 (September 1993), pp. 1263–89, shows that a common failing of predictions of the effects of deregulation is to underestimate the intensity of competition and improvements in service quality and to overstate the extent to which certain consumers are likely to be hurt by a change to unregulated competition.

Objections to Privatization

There are, of course, serious practical objections to privatizing transit. In the first place, before federal involvement in urban transit began in the 1960s the United States had been there and done that—without success. But Peter Pashigian and George Hilton, among others, have argued that regulatory constraints seriously hampered the performance of private bus companies and that private operations could have succeeded.[14] Indeed, the private systems that operate today still face regulatory restrictions on their operations. Suburban private operations have begun to offer service once provided by large public systems and have produced encouraging results.[15] And bus deregulation in Britain, although controversial, has generally produced enough net benefits to the British public to raise proposals to privatize London's subway system.[16] Indeed, the initial effects of British bus deregulation parallel our short-run predictions of the effects of privatization. Public subsidies have decreased significantly as costs have fallen and fares have risen, and minibuses have emerged as a major form of service innovation, which has increased vehicle miles. Bus ridership has generally declined in response to higher fares, but some areas of the country have experienced increases in ridership in response to intensive

14. Peter Pashigian, "Consequences and Causes of Public Ownership of Urban Transit Facilities," *Journal of Political Economy*, vol. 84 (December 1976), pp. 1239–59; and George W. Hilton, "The Rise and Fall of Monopolized Transit," in Lave, *Urban Transit*, pp. 31–48.

15. See, for example, Stephen C. Fehr, "Metrobus Losing Money and Muscle: Cheaper Suburban Transit Is Devastating the Regional System, Officials Fear," *Washington Post*, April 3, 1994, p. A1. Alice Reid, "Metro Aims to Increase Ridership," *Washington Post*, September 26, 1997, p. B1, reports that a regional panel recommended that private companies should run more of the Washington area's local and neighborhood buses, leaving Metro to run regional routes. A new bus plan for the Washington metropolitan area, which will make greater use of private operations, is scheduled to be phased in beginning in 1999.

16. José A. Gomez-Ibañez and John R. Meyer, "Privatizing and Deregulating Local Public Services: Lessons from Britain's Buses," *Journal of the American Planning Association*, vol. 56 (Winter 1990), pp. 9–21, provide a favorable overall assessment of British bus deregulation. T. R. Reid, "Sprucing Up London's Seedy Tube," *Washington Post*, March 21, 1998, points out that the Conservative party wanted to sell the London subway system to a private company. Prime Minister Tony Blair's labor government has proposed a public-private partnership, with a public entity running the trains but private companies given interest in tracks, rolling stock, signals, and so on, and charging rent to the public transit authority for use of renewed facilities. Other countries, such as the Netherlands, are currently considering proposals to privatize their public transport systems. For a complete discussion of the international experience see Gomez-Ibañez and Meyer, *Going Private*.

urban minibus operations, which may bode well for the long-run effects of this policy.[17]

Transit union leaders often resist efforts by a city to allow more private service because they want to protect the high wages and employment security of their members. With train operators and station agents for the BART system in San Francisco, for example, being paid more than $40,000 a year, this self-interest is understandable.[18] But the economic effects that privatization would have on the transit labor force are not entirely clear. Although it is likely that labor would experience reductions in wages, it is conceivable that an efficient private transit industry could actually generate an increase in patronage and provide more transit employment.

Other opponents of transit privatization claim that any efficiency gains will be accompanied by a redistribution of income from low- or fixed-income travelers to wealthier citizens. But as we found in chapter 5, the elderly and the economically disadvantaged are not the primary beneficiaries of the fares and service provided by the public transit system. In fact, Richard Crepeau and Charles Lave have found that the presence or absence of transit makes little difference in the mobility patterns of the elderly.[19] And programs such as reverse commuting, which are designed to give low-income people greater access to suburban jobs, have not met with great success.[20]

In general, research has concluded that there may be a link between poverty and accessibility but that government experiments to raise the living standards of poor people by improving the quality of public transit have been unsuccessful.[21] Car pools, low-cost vans, and so on may be more

17. Peter White, "Deregulation of Local Bus Services in Great Britain: An Introductory Review," *Transport Reviews*, vol. 15, no. 2 (1995), pp. 185–209.

18. Richard Price, "S. F. Transit Strikers Get Little Sympathy," *USA Today*, September 10, 1997.

19. Richard Crepeau and Charles Lave, "Travel by Carless Households,"*ACCESS: University of California Institute of Transportation Studies Magazine*, no. 9 (Fall 1996), pp. 29– 31.

20. Stephen Blake, *Inner City Minority Transit Needs in Accessing Suburban Employment Centers* (Washington: National Association of Regional Councils, 1989), points out that it is much more important for inner-city residents to be able to retain jobs than to have greater accessibility to them.

21. Katherine M. O'Regan and John M. Quigley, "Accessibility and Economic Opportunity," in José A. Gomez-Ibañez, William B. Tye, and Clifford Winston, eds., *Essays in Transportation Economics and Policy: A Handbook in Honor of John R. Meyer* (Brookings, forthcoming).

effective than full-size conventional buses at serving dispersed suburban workplaces.

A more fundamental problem with public transit systems is that they have difficulty keeping up with and responding to changes in job growth and demographics. To the extent that these systems create new routes, they mainly focus on commuting professionals heading toward the central business district, not on lower-income residents who either live in or want access to employment opportunities in outlying suburbs, or on retired citizens who want access to leisure activities.[22] Future public transportation prospects for the poor are dim as long as financial pressures force public transit systems to continue to cut routes and political pressures force them to resist serving low-income areas.[23]

A compelling example of the potential benefits that privatization could provide to low-income workers is the Queens Van Plan, a private company that serves mostly low- to middle-income minority workers in New York's Queens and Nassau counties. Because its customers live in areas neglected by public mass transit, the Queens Van Plan provides an indispensable service and operates at a profit while charging only a dollar a ride. Current regulations, however, prevent the company from offering service in other low-income areas of New York. In fact, it has filed a suit against the state and city of New York to be allowed to expand its service.[24] Under a privatized system, Queens Van Plan and similar companies would be free to provide inexpensive service to any low-income neighborhood.

22. The failure of public transit to provide access to jobs in the outer suburbs of Washington, D.C., is described by Sewell Chan, "Where a Car Is Key to Survival," *Washington Post*, July 21, 1997, p. B1, and its failure to provide access to jobs in the outer suburbs of New York is described by Jane Gross, "Poor without Cars Find Trek to Work Can Be a Job," *New York Times*, November 18, 1997, p. A1. Its failure to provide access to jobs in the Detroit suburbs is described by Robyn Meredith, "Jobs Out of Reach for Detroiters without Wheels," *New York Times*, May 26, 1998, p. A12. The failure of public transportation to provide alternative means of access to leisure activities for retired citizens who have stopped driving is described by Sara Rimer, "An Aging Nation Ill-Equipped for Hanging Up the Car Keys," *New York Times*, December 15, 1997, p. A1.

23. This problem is already developing in some areas of the country as new laws push people off welfare and into the work force. For example, as reported by Alice Reid, "For Many New Hires, Getting There Is Half the Battle," *Washington Post*, December 23, 1996, p. B1, many poor people in and around Washington, D.C., are finding that public transit does not serve areas that are potential places of employment.

24. See Hector Ricketts, "Roadblocks Made Just for Vans," *New York Times*, November 22, 1997, p. A15.

Given the continuing failures of public transit to serve the interests of the poor and the restrictions placed on those companies that wish to do so, it is not likely that privatization will hurt low-income travelers more than other travelers. In fact, as in the case of intercity transportation deregulation, it may actually improve their welfare.[25]

The Transition

Notwithstanding its name, the objective of privatization is to promote competition, not simply to replace public companies with private ones. The mechanisms that have been commonly advocated to promote competition in urban transit include increasing contractual arrangements with private companies and relaxing controls on market entry.[26]

We see both mechanisms as important first steps, but we believe that the country's recent experience with economic deregulation suggests that if privatization is to succeed, policymakers' ultimate objective should be to have all transit service provided by private companies with no restrictions, or very few, on fares and market entry. For bus transportation, authorities could initially contract with private entrepreneurs to provide service, allowing these newly formed companies to make pricing and service decisions with the objective of making a competitive rate of return.[27] New companies would be allowed to enter the market within a designated time frame without any restrictions on their prices and service, at which time the companies that were operating under contract should become fully responsible for

25. Winston, "U.S. Industry Adjustment to Economic Deregulation." As with intercity transportation deregulation, third parties, whether they be employers, cities, or marketing entities, could negotiate with private transit firms to achieve lower fares and improved service for low-income travelers.

26. Lave, ed., *Urban Transit*.

27. Gomez-Ibañez and Meyer, *Going Private*, point out that Santiago, Chile, allowed its publicly owned bus company to disband when it privatized bus operations and relaxed fare and route regulations on private operators. This approach may be inappropriate for U.S. cities that have large public systems because private bus operations account for a small share of riders in these cities. Klein, Moore, and Reja, *Curb Rights*, suggest a property rights approach to improving transit that would enable private jitneys to compete with scheduled transit service. Policymakers could also experiment with curb rights as a first step to realizing the benefits from unregulated private competition.

acquiring and maintaining their transit capital stock and free to set any prices and enter any routes that they wish.

The transition to private competitive rail service may appear formidable because of the huge capital requirements involved in building and maintaining a rail network. But the same principles used to guide the transition to competition in bus transportation can also guide the transition to competition in rail transportation. Again transit authorities could contract with private entrepreneurs to provide rail service designed to make a competitive rate of return. At the same time, the authorities should begin to develop plans to sell the rail network to either one company or several that would each own part of the network.[28] In all likelihood, access charges would have to be agreed upon to give prospective entrants the opportunity to provide service. Although we do not want to minimize the importance of a well-managed bidding process to transfer ownership to private rail companies and the difficulty and length of the transition to develop private sector transit competition, we are confident that if the United States can have a competitive and reasonably profitable private rail freight system, there is no reason that it cannot have a viable private urban rail transit system.[29]

The federal government should encourage cities to run privatization experiments, although the cities should be free to find their own way to introduce private sector competition in transit and reduce their system's dependence on taxpayer support.[30] To be sure, it will take time for businesses and travelers to adjust to the new competitive order. And notwithstanding our arguments that in the long run privatization is not likely to cost low-income travelers more, some assurances, perhaps through a trans-

28. As discussed by Louis Thompson and Karim-Jacques Budin, "Railway Concessions: Progress to Date," World Bank report, January 1998, the transition to private rail could involve "concessions," which would consist of continuing public ownership and oversight of rail infrastructure but operating responsibility and the delivery of services transferred to the private sector.

29. One might wonder whether the country could have a competitive and profitable intercity rail passenger system. Rail intercity passenger transportation is at a severe cost disadvantage against automobiles for short trips and at a severe time disadvantage against air transportation for medium- to long-distance trips. Thus even an efficient private sector intercity rail system would probably be economically viable only on short trips in high-density corridors. Urban rail transit would obviously compete for short trips and would have the opportunity to achieve sufficient passenger density, especially by aligning vehicle capacity with demand by using only a few rail cars if necessary, in many urban areas of the country.

30. Formula grants, for example, could be used to encourage these experiments.

portation voucher program, that they will not be worse off should help gain support for the experiments. But once privatization experiments are initiated, policymakers must allow competition to develop and not attempt to micromanage.

Private Roads

Congestion continues to be the most urgent problem confronting automobile travel, and congestion tolls represent the most efficient solution. A partial solution to congestion has undoubtedly occurred without changing how roads are priced because those people who value travel time most highly reduce their costs from congestion by, for example, living closer to work or in less congested cities.[31] Thus the direct benefits from congestion pricing to those travelers who might actually benefit from it are currently not large enough for any policymaker to justify the losses that most automobile travelers would experience from paying tolls.

In the long run, however, congestion pricing could lead to more efficient residential and business locations. That is, the adjustments people and businesses make to avoid congestion and the resulting distortions in land prices do generate costs: some people live closer to work than optimal, others live further from work than optimal, and so on. And these costs are not simply transfers of wealth. Inefficient road pricing contributes to urban sprawl and the loss of economies from urban density. Although we are not aware of quantitative estimates of these costs, they could be large and widespread and, by themselves, justify policymakers' support for congestion pricing.

Theory aside, there has been minimal interest in implementing congestion pricing on public roads.[32] But at long last, congestion tolls have been

31. John Calfee and Clifford Winston, "The Value of Automobile Travel Time: Implications for Congestion Policy," *Journal of Public Economics,* vol. 69 (July 1998), pp. 83–102.

32. As noted in chapter 5, Congress approved a congestion pricing demonstration project for the San Francisco Bay Bridge, but it was never implemented. An electronic toll lane has recently been introduced on the Triborough Bridge in New York. The New York Metropolitan Transportation Authority is studying the feasibility of using electronic toll technology to introduce congestion pricing. In Southern California from Riverside County to Orange County, rush hour solo commuters can pay a fee to have access to a less congested high-vehicle-occupancy toll (HOT) lane. HOT lanes are also in use in San Diego and Houston.

introduced in the United States on a private highway in Orange County, California. Every workday 24,000 drivers pay as much as $2.75 a trip to avoid the congested state route. Apparently, these commuters are unable (or unwilling) to reside where they can avoid congestion. The California Private Transportation Company, which owns the road, is so enthusiastic about the results that it is looking for opportunities to build similar ones.[33] A series of successful experiments with congestion tolls on private roads, either in California or elsewhere, could spur adoption of tolls on more highways throughout the country.[34]

It is also conceivable that government will eventually adopt congestion pricing. *The Economist* suggests that congestion pricing is already starting to appear throughout the world in accordance with the number of vehicles a country has per kilometer of road.[35] Thus it is not surprising that Singapore, Japan, and some west European countries have shown more interest in road pricing (Singapore has actually adopted it) than have the United States and Canada. It is also not surprising that Los Angeles is the first city in the United States to consider a proposal to partly convert its freeways into toll roads by letting solo commuters pay to use existing car pool lanes.[36]

An alternative view is that it is not worth waiting for government to someday get around to adopting congestion pricing and that policymakers should give serious consideration to privatizing U.S. highways.[37] A rigorous

33. Kim Clark, "How to Make Traffic Jams a Thing of the Past," *Fortune*, March 31, 1997, p. 34. Philip A. Viton, "Private Roads," *Journal of Urban Economics*, vol. 37 (May 1995), pp. 260–89, has developed a model in which private toll-supported roads compete directly with free public expressways and finds that the private roads can succeed financially under widely varying circumstances.

34. The Dulles-Greenway toll road outside Washington, D.C., has had to lower its toll significantly to attract ridership and cover its debt service. But part of the explanation for its financial problems may be that people who put a high value on their time live closer to the city. Thus the toll road's potential customers are not willing to pay to save travel time and are content to use untolled alternative routes that are available and that do not take much more time than the toll road.

35. "Living with the Car," *Economist*, December 6, 1997, pp. 21–23.

36. Other metropolitan areas, such as Washington, D.C., have recently announced that they are considering proposals to let solo drivers pay a toll to use carpool lanes.

37. The greater Los Angeles area has produced a plan that involves private financing of truck tollways. The thinking is that truck operators would pay tolls to bypass congestion on untolled freeways.

treatment of this idea is beyond the scope of this book, but the basic issues can be sketched. According to Gabriel Roth, the economic performance of public roads—highways operate at a loss and make inefficient use of their capacity—is similar to the economic performance of public transit.[38] Kenneth Small, Clifford Winston, and Carol Evans have also pointed out that highway durability is not what it should be, which increases maintenance costs.[39] The source of these problems is inefficient pricing, investment, and maintenance. Advocates of privatization argue that these inefficiencies will be reduced only if roads are subjected to competitive forces—that is, owned and operated by private commercial companies that must compete with other companies and modes of transportation. New Zealand is apparently giving this idea serious thought, because it is considering a proposal in which government road assets would be given to commercial road companies. These companies would then be expected to charge for road use and to earn a return on capital, while being treated for regulatory purposes as (monopoly) businesses.

Is it appropriate for the United States to consider this step? In the absence of accumulated empirical evidence, we believe it is premature to recommend privatization of U.S. highways. One obvious concern is that public authorities are likely to regulate tolls and they may discourage efficient pricing schemes. We recognize, however, that privatization could become more attractive as road technology evolves. Many transportation engineers and planners envision highway travel that is characterized by sophisticated navigational aids to guide route choices, set travel speeds, and even drive the vehicle itself. But these technological advances will call for greater management of highway travel. In fact, "road traffic control" is likely to become as essential to ground transportation as air traffic control is to air transportation. The potential economic concern is that management of a sophisticated and technologically advanced road system by a govern-

---

38. Roth, *Roads in a Market Economy,* p. 16. Recent annual highway losses are estimated at $6 billion.

39. Kenneth A. Small, Clifford Winston, and Carol A. Evans, *Road Work: A New Highway Pricing and Investment Policy* (Brookings, 1989), contend that roads do not have optimal lifetimes because their pavements are too thin and truck user charges, based on the fuel tax, do not accord with the damage that a truck does to a road, which depends on a truck's axle weight.

ment agency could turn out to be as inefficient as Federal Aviation Administration management of air traffic control and prompt familiar calls for a private road traffic control system.[40] To avoid the inefficiencies of a public road traffic control system and the transition costs of developing a private sytem, it could become desirable in the long run to privatize the highway system and have each company be responsible for implementing and managing technological advances in road travel.

A strong argument for privatization and deregulation in transportation has been that the government has thwarted technological advance and mismanaged the advances that have been introduced. As we prepare to enter a more advanced era of highway transportation, this fundamental argument may apply with greater force.

Deregulation of Taxi Operations

Policymakers seeking to stimulate competition in urban transportation should also consider deregulating taxicabs nationwide. Researchers have found mixed effects in the twenty or so U.S. urbanized areas that have deregulated taxi fares and market entry and exit.[41] Fares have decreased and service quality has improved in some cities, while fares have risen and service quality has deteriorated in others. On average, our data suggest that, controlling for operating environments, fares are slightly higher and taxi availability (number of taxis) is slightly lower in those cities that have deregulated fares and market entry. Although enthusiasm for taxi deregulation is not widespread, recent deregulations in Denver, Indianapolis, and

40. The Federal Aviation Administration has been criticized for decades for maintaining an inefficient and outdated air traffic control system. The National Civil Aviation Review Commission has investigated these concerns and recently recommended partial privatization of the FAA. It also called for the airline industry to increase its self-regulation instead of relying so heavily on federal enforcement and safety rules.

41. In some of these areas, fares are required to be posted. Mark W. Frankena and Paul A. Pautler, "Taxicab Regulation: An Economic Analysis," *Research in Law and Economics*, vol. 9 (1986), pp. 129–65, provide a complete assessment of taxi deregulation. Klein, Moore, and Reja, *Curb Rights,* provide a recent discussion.

Cincinnati have led to more taxi service, which provides some support for the idea.[42]

Taxi deregulation is likely to be most beneficial if it is part of a broader policy to stimulate competition in urban transportation. For example, deregulation of freight transportation as a whole has forced railroads and trucking companies to become more efficient and responsive to shippers. The carriers can no longer assume that any traffic is theirs alone and have thus developed a range of services to meet shippers' specialized requirements. Some of these involve efficient truck-rail operations. Faced with competition from revitalized transit companies, taxis will no longer occupy a safe niche between the private car and the city bus or rail service. They will be forced to compete with some transit services such as vans that operate like taxis and also offer intermodal services with rail and bus operations. The increased intermodal competition and coordination in a privatized and deregulated urban transportation system should lower taxi fares, improve service quality, and enable taxi operations to provide some competitive discipline for transit.

Conclusion

Policymakers are likely to improve the efficiency of urban transportation only if they are rewarded—that is, reelected—on grounds unrelated to their service to certain travelers and suppliers. Politics being politics, however, that is not going to happen. As an alternative, we contend that allowing the private sector to become an important factor in providing urban transportation would strongly improve its efficiency and could meet objections to its political practicality.

Of course, it is difficult to predict very accurately what a privatized system would look like, but in an environment where travelers have the ability and incentive to act on their preferences and where operators have the ability and incentive to respond to these preferences, the U.S. urban transportation system would offer a broader and more efficient range of

42. See William Mellor, "Free-Enterprise Cabs," *Washington Post,* January 8, 1997, p. A24.

services than it currently offers. Large employers could negotiate reliable high-volume commuter services; school buses could double up on commuter runs for residents in low-density areas; vans, jitneys, and taxis could provide low-cost service to low-income travelers; and intermodal operations could benefit all travelers. We recognize that the transition to privatization would be unsettling and could possibly generate loud and fierce criticism. We therefore recommend that policymakers promote privatization experiments in selected urban areas and provide a safety net for low-income travelers.

7

Conclusion

W E BEGAN this book with an examination question that asked how economic analysis can help eliminate the inefficiencies that pervade urban transportation in the United States. Our first answer—improve transit operating efficiency and set prices and service levels to maximize net benefits—and our empirical evidence for the recommendation—the annual net benefits from this policy would be considerably more than $10 billion (1990) dollars a year—should satisfy academic examiners and would-be examiners, but they are unlikely to pique the interest of policymakers. The efficiency costs of subsidized prices and inefficient service are a consequence of urban transportation policies that political forces have forged into tools for redistributing income from taxpayers to suppliers and certain travelers, the majority of whom cannot be characterized as economically disadvantaged.

Because these political forces are unlikely to change, we have offered a second and, in our view, more constructive answer: the only possible way for policymakers to significantly improve the efficiency of urban transportation and the welfare of the economically disadvantaged traveler is to relinquish most of their economic decisionmaking authority by privatizing urban transit, encouraging the development of private toll roads, and deregulating taxis.

Is it realistic to believe that those entities that decide transportation issues would consider such a fundamental change in policy? To answer that question, one must understand why urban transportation is largely provided by the public sector and under what conditions policymakers would allow private companies to take greater responsibility for it. The economic theory of regulation argues that urban transportation is provided by the public sector because those interests that stand to gain the most from public provision—transit managers, unions, contractors, and certain travelers—have "captured" policymakers. Of course, capture is not a one-way street because policymakers do get rewarded by campaign contributions, votes, and power. Thus, privatization becomes an attractive option when the costs to policymakers of public provision, that is, the efficiency losses from political patronage, exceed the benefits.[1]

The losses in urban transportation are sizable and increasing, and all levels of government have felt pressure to reduce the growth in transportation spending. Thus the prospects for greater private sector involvement appear promising. But the recent improvement in the federal budget and the budgets of some states relieves some of the pressure to cut transportation spending, and new federal legislation substantially increases spending on urban transportation over the next several years. Thus public pressure to curb transportation subsidies may not yet provide sufficient benefits to politicians to offset the political costs.

Nonetheless, the budgetary improvements and increased transportation spending do not change the evidence in this book that calls for a fundamental rethinking about the way urban transportation is provided in America. Eventually, the political cost of an urban transportation system characterized by large deficits and deteriorating performance will spur policy change. The few market experiments in urban transportation that are in the planning stages offer a glimpse of the potential benefits we have discussed. Our hope is that policymakers will find it in their interest to act sooner rather than later and encourage further experiments to expedite private sector involvement in providing urban transportation.

1. Florencio Lopez-de-Silanes, Andrei Shleifer, and Robert W. Vishny, "Privatization in the United States," *Rand Journal of Economics*, vol. 28 (Autumn 1997), pp. 447–71, have investigated the determinants of privatization in the United States and presented empirical evidence that is generally consistent with that proposition.

Appendix A
Average Automobile Speeds

THIS APPENDIX describes how we estimated average speeds for the automobile modes and the distribution of commuters' mileage on local roads and highways. Auto speeds were derived for local roads and highways using speed-flow curves, which describe the relationship between the density of traffic and the speeds at which traffic flows.

Based on the work of Siamak Ardekani and Robert Herman, the speeds S for local roads are given by

$$S = 18.38 \, [1 - (0.01 \, D/W)^{1.239}]^{2.58},$$

where D is vehicle traffic density, and W is the number of lanes.[1]

Based on the work of Theodore Keeler and Kenneth Small, the speeds S for highways are given by

$$S = 46 \pm \sqrt{2{,}111 - 520.1 \, [(V/C) + 3.153]} \, ,$$

where V is vehicle traffic volume per lane per hour and C is freeway lane capacity.[2] We used Keeler and Small's peaking ratios (a peaking ratio is the ratio of traffic during a given time period to traffic during an average hour of the day) to allocate daily traffic volumes to different travel periods

1. Siamak Ardekani and Robert Herman, "Urban Network-Wide Traffic Variables and Their Relations," *Transportation Science*, vol. 21 (1987), pp. 1–16.
2. Theodore E. Keeler and Kenneth A. Small, "Optimal Peak-Load Pricing, Investment, and Service Levels on Urban Expressways," *Journal of Political Economy*, vol. 85 (January 1977), pp. 1–25.

throughout the day. Although these ratios are somewhat dated, we have not seen more recent data that seriously question the use of them here.

We also estimated the distribution of commuters' mileage on local roads and highways. Because we did not have any information on travelers' route choices, we obtained the distribution of miles on highways and local roads by taking the average trip distance, travel time, and speeds of the traffic flow on local roads and highways to compute the mileage the average commuter must have covered on each type of road to achieve the average commuting time.[3] We typically found that commuting distances were equally divided between highway and local mileage.

3. Average trip distances and travel times were obtained from the 1990 Census of Population and Housing.

Appendix B
Means for Modal Attributes, by Commuting Distance

APPENDIX table B-1 presents the means for the modal attributes by commute distance block. These means correspond to the mode and departure-time choice parameter estimates presented in table 3-2 in the text.

Table B-1. *Means of Modal Attributes, by Distance Block*

Attribute	Drive alone	Car pool	Bus	Rail	Taxi
		Distance block 1: less than 1 mile			
Fare per mile/annual household income (defined for 7:30–9:00 a.m., 0 otherwise)	0.0000076	0.0000031	0.0000215	0.0000263	0.0000395
Fare per mile/annual household income (defined for other than 7:30–9:00 a.m., 0 otherwise)	0.0000076	0.0000031	0.0000215	0.0000263	0.0000395
Total travel time per mile/annual household income (defined for 7:30–9:00 a.m., 0 otherwise)	0.0000691	0.0003060	0.0007651	0.0002738	0.0000691
Total travel time per mile/annual household income (defined for other than 7:30–9:00 a.m., 0 otherwise)	0.0000611	0.0002977	0.0008162	0.0004002	0.0000611
Route coverage (road or route miles per square mile of urbanized area)	9.74	9.74	2.59	0.10	9.74
Peak period (6:30–9:00 a.m.) frequency of service (thousands of daily vehicle miles per road or route mile)[a]	5.026	5.026	0.038	0.929	5.026
Off-peak period (times other than 6:30–9:00 a.m.) frequency of service (thousands of daily vehicle miles per road or route mile)[a]	5.026	5.026	0.022	0.499	5.026

Distance block 2: 1–5 miles

Fare per mile/annual household income (defined for 7:30–9:00 a.m., 0 otherwise)	0.0000076	0.0000031	0.0000035	0.0000045	0.0000360
Fare per mile/annual household income (defined for other than 7:30–9:00 a.m., 0 otherwise)	0.0000076	0.0000031	0.0000035	0.0000045	0.0000360
Total travel time per mile/annual household income (defined for 7:30–9:00 a.m., 0 otherwise)	0.0000691	0.0001096	0.0002189	0.0001214	0.0000691
Total travel time per mile/annual household income (defined for other than 7:30–9:00 a.m., 0 otherwise)	0.0000611	0.0001013	0.0002274	0.0001429	0.0000611
Route coverage (road or route miles per square mile of urbanized area)	9.74	9.74	2.59	0.10	9.74
Peak period (6:30–9:00 a.m.) frequency of service (thousands of daily vehicle miles per road or route mile)[a]	5.026	5.026	0.038	0.929	5.026
Off-peak period (times other than 6:30–9:00 a.m.) frequency of service (thousands of daily vehicle miles per road or route mile)[a]	5.026	5.026	0.022	0.499	5.026

(continued)

Table B-1. *Means of Modal Attributes, by Distance Block (Continued)*

Attribute	Drive alone	Car pool	Bus	Rail	Taxi
			Distance block 3: 6–10 miles		
Fare per mile/annual household income (defined for 7:30–9:00 a.m., 0 otherwise)	0.0000076	0.0000031	0.0000014	0.0000019	0.0000355
Fare per mile/annual household income (defined for other than 7:30–9:00 a.m., 0 otherwise)	0.0000076	0.0000031	0.0000014	0.0000019	0.0000355
Total travel time per mile/annual household income (defined for 7:30–9:00 a.m., 0 otherwise)	0.0000691	0.0000857	0.0001519	0.0001029	0.0000691
Total travel time per mile/annual household income (defined for other than 7:30–9:00 a.m., 0 otherwise)	0.0000611	0.0000774	0.0001555	0.0000970	0.0000611
Route coverage (road or route miles per square mile of urbanized area)	9.74	9.74	2.59	0.10	9.74
Peak period (6:30–9:00 a.m.) frequency of service (thousands of daily vehicle miles per road or route mile)[a]	5.026	5.026	0.038	0.929	5.026
Off-peak period (times other than 6:30–9:00 a.m.) frequency of service (thousands of daily vehicle miles per road or route mile)[a]	5.026	5.026	0.022	0.499	5.026

Fare per mile/annual household income (defined for 7:30–9:00 a.m., 0 otherwise)	0.0000076	0.0000031	0.0000007	0.0000009	0.0000355
Fare per mile/annual household income (defined for other than 7:30–9:00 a.m., 0 otherwise)	0.0000076	0.0000031	0.0000007	0.0000009	0.0000355
Total travel time per mile/annual household income (defined for 7:30–9:00 a.m., 0 otherwise)	0.0000691	0.0000816	0.0001283	0.0000963	0.0000691
Total travel time per mile/annual household income (defined for other than 7:30–9:00 a.m., 0 otherwise)	0.0000611	0.0000736	0.0001302	0.0001006	0.0000611
Route coverage (road or route miles per square mile of urbanized area)	9.74	9.74	2.59	0.10	9.74
Peak period (6:30–9:00 a.m.) frequency of service (thousands of daily vehicle miles per road or route mile)[a]	5.026	5.026	0.038	0.929	5.026
Off-peak period (times other than 6:30–9:00 a.m.) frequency of service (thousands of daily vehicle miles per road or route mile)[a]	5.026	5.026	0.022	0.499	5.026

(continued)

Table B-1. *Means of Modal Attributes, by Distance Block (Continued)*

Attribute	Drive alone	Car pool	Bus	Rail	Taxi
		Distance block 5: more than 25 miles			
Fare per mile/annual household income (defined for 7:30–9:00 a.m., 0 otherwise)	0.0000076	0.0000031	0.0000002	0.0000002	0.0000353
Fare per mile/annual household income (defined for other than 7:30–9:00 a.m., 0 otherwise)	0.0000076	0.0000031	0.0000002	0.0000002	0.0000353
Total travel time per mile/annual household income (defined for 7:30–9:00 a.m., 0 otherwise)	0.0000691	0.0000741	0.0001148	0.0000857	0.0000691
Total travel time per mile/annual household income (defined for other than 7:30–9:00 a.m., 0 otherwise)	0.0000611	0.0000658	0.0001150	0.0000864	0.0000611
Route coverage (road or route miles per square mile of urbanized area)	9.74	9.74	2.59	0.10	9.74
Peak period (6:30–9:00 a.m.) frequency of service (thousands of daily vehicle miles per road or route mile)[a]	5.026	5.026	0.038	0.929	5.026
Off-peak period (times other than 6:30–9:00 a.m.) frequency of service (thousands of daily vehicle miles per road or route mile)[a]	5.026	5.026	0.022	0.499	5.026

a. As described in the text, transit frequencies are scaled during the day to account for their greater frequency during peak hours.

Appendix C
Parameter Estimates of
Rail Attribute Equations

THIS APPENDIX presents the three-stage least squares parameter estimates of the rail attribute equations. As with buses, the parameter estimates indicate that the determinants of rail attributes go beyond conventional economic influences to include government subsidies, policymaking entities, and constituents (table C-1).[1]

Rail Fare Equation

Rail fares are influenced in plausible ways by economic variables. Greater trip distances and population densities increase rail fares, while economies from greater route density reduce fares. Government subsidies also reduce fares.

Local entities, either directly or through the transit authority that they appoint, do not promote rail because fares are higher when these entities are responsible for fare decisions. There appear to be federal "patrons" of urban rail, as there are of intercity rail (Amtrak), because rail fares fall when the number of Democratic senators in a state increases. Rail fares also respond, but in conflicting ways, to different constituencies. Fares tend to fall as the shares of lower-income and upper middle-income rail riders expand, but rise as the share of lower middle-income riders expands.

---

1. Estimations were based on urbanized areas that had rail systems. We did not find any appreciable improvements from jointly estimating an urbanized area's rail and bus attribute equations.

Table C-1. *Three-Stage Least Squares Estimates of Rail Attribute Equations*[a]

Variable	Coefficient
Rail fare equation	
Constant	0.3915
	(0.0548)
Average rail work trip distance (miles)	0.0360
	(0.0065)
Population density in principal central city (population per square mile)	0.1868E-04
	(0.3511E-05)
Route coverage (directional rail route miles per square mile in UZA)	–0.5508
	(0.2271)
Subsidy (nonpassenger fare revenue per maximum-service vehicle, thousands of dollars per vehicle)	–0.1674E-04
	(0.2023E-05)
City makes fare decisions (1 if city makes decisions, 0 otherwise)	0.2035
	(0.0227)
City-appointed transit authority makes fare decisions (1 if city-appointed transit authority makes decisions, 0 otherwise)	0.2345
	(0.0282)
Number of Democratic senators in state	–0.1278
	(0.0197)
Lower-income rail commuters as percent of persons older than 16	–175.380
	(35.221)
Upper middle-income rail commuters as percent of persons older than 16	–86.319
	(20.572)
Lower middle-income rail commuters as percent of persons older than 16	104.288
	(22.219)
Rail route coverage equation	
Constant	0.0084
	(0.0175)
Population density in principal central city (population per square mile)	0.4485E-05
	(0.2222E-05
Popularly appointed transit authority makes route decisions (1 if popularly appointed transit authority makes decisions, 0 otherwise)	–0.0114
	(0.0079)
Governor-appointed transit authority makes route decisions (1 if governor-appointed transit authority makes decisions, 0 otherwise)	–0.0182
	(0.0074)
Local entity receives federal mass transit grant money (1 if local entity receives grant money, 0 otherwise)	0.0494
	(0.0103)

(continued)

Table C-1. *Three-Stage Least Squares Estimates of Rail Attribute Equations*[a]
(Continued)

Variable	Coefficient
Rail route coverage equation (continued)	
Upper middle-income rail commuters as percent of persons older than 16	53.301
	(9.286)
Asian-American rail commuters as percent of persons older than 16	8.807
	(4.149)
Lower-income rail commuters as percent of persons older than 16	−26.634
	(3.794)
Upper-income rail commuters as percent of persons older than 16	−40.043
	(7.766)
Rail frequency equation	
Constant	325.163
	(75.55)
Population density in principal central city (population per square mile)	0.0336
	(0.0070)
Operating expense per passenger mile (dollars per passenger mile)	−37.346
	(12.029)
Route coverage (directional rail route miles per square mile in UZA)	−2440.29
	(579.67)
Subsidy (nonpassenger fare revenue per maximum-service vehicle, thousands of dollars per vehicle)	0.0239
	(0.0098)
Governor-appointed transit authority makes route decisions (1 if governor-appointed transit authority makes decisions, 0 otherwise)	116.493
	(88.139)
Local entity makes route decisions (1 if local entity makes decisions, 0 otherwise)	−162.73
	(50.45)
Upper middle-income rail commuters as percent of persons older than 16	46879.1
	(15091.6)
Lower middle-income rail commuters as percent of persons older than 16	−22546.2
	(10960.3)
R^2 of rail fare equation	0.95
R^2 of rail route coverage equation	0.93
R^2 of rail frequency equation	0.83

Source: Authors' calculations; and see table 5-1.
a. White heteroskedastic standard errors are in parentheses.

Route Coverage Equation

Route coverage seems primarily determined by noneconomic influences. As with bus transportation, the only statistically reliable economic effect we found was that greater population density leads to greater route coverage. Transit authorities, whether popularly elected or appointed by the governor, tend to curtail route coverage, while local entities that receive federal transit money tend to expand it.

Route coverage grows as the proportion of upper middle-income riders increases, thus providing more evidence that well-off suburban commuters especially benefit from these systems. Increases in the proportion of Asian-American riders also expand route coverage. But increases in the share of lower- and upper-income riders curtail route coverage.[2]

Rail Frequency Equation

As with bus transportation, economic considerations play a greater part in determining frequency of rail service than in determining route coverage. Increased population density increases frequency, while greater operating expenses and broader route coverage decrease it. Government subsidies increase frequency.

Some policymaking entities have distinct effects on frequency. Governor-appointed transit authorities tend to increase it, but local entities decrease it. Again, upper middle-income riders clearly benefit from urban rail systems because frequency increases when their share of patronage increases. Frequency decreases, however, when the share of lower middle-income riders increases.

2. In the case of bus service, we suggested that the finding that increases in the share of black and Hispanic riders curtailed route coverage could reflect the resistance that some communities have toward expanding route coverage because of their fear of attracting more crime. The relevant crime "signal" for rail route coverage may simply be income rather than race, which may explain the negative sign for lower-income travelers. Higher-income travelers may prefer a smaller system for this reason, provided they have access to the urban areas where they engage in work and leisure activities.

Appendix D: Sources of the Welfare Loss from Transit, Based on Generalized Least Squares Estimation

ESTIMATES of the sources of the welfare loss from transit operations are presented in table D-1, which is based on attribute equations that were estimated by generalized least squares. The findings are generally consistent with those presented in the text based on attribute equations that were estimated by three-stage least squares.

Table D-1. *Source of Welfare Loss Based on Attribute Equations Estimated by Generalized Least Squares*

Percent unless otherwise specified

Influence that is eliminated	Change in bus		Change in rail		Welfare improvement (millions of dollars)
	Fare	Frequency	Fare	Frequency	
Subsidies	14.6	−14.4	12.1	−30.6	1,390
Local decisionmaking entities	28.2	−12.3	−8.2	24.9	620
Governor-appointed transit authorities	2.4	−3.8	0	−25.8	900
Consitituents (socioeconomic and ethnic groups)	−10.7	−38.3	−1.0	−9.9	2,970

Source: Authors' calculations.

Index